CAMBRIDGE LIBRARY COLLECTION

Books of enduring scholarly value

Religion

For centuries, scripture and theology were the focus of prodigious amounts
of scholarship and publishing, dominated in the English-speaking world
by the work of Protestant Christians. Enlightenment philosophy and
science, anthropology, ethnology and the colonial experience all brought
new perspectives, lively debates and heated controversies to the study of
religion and its role in the world, many of which continue to this day. This
series explores the editing and interpretation of religious texts, the history of
religious ideas and institutions, and not least the encounter between religion
and science.

The Theology of an Evolutionist

A Congregationalist clergyman, editor of the influential progressive journal
The Outlook, and intimate with Henry Ward Beecher and Theodore Roosevelt,
Lyman Abbott (1835–1922) played a central role in religion and politics in
turn-of-the-century America. In this work, first published in 1897, Abbott
shows his characteristic optimism in human moral development, arguing
that the Christian faith can fully accommodate evolution as the means by
which God changes and improves the world over time. Abbott writes 'not to
disbelievers in evolution to prove that they are mistaken, but to believers in
evolution to show them that their belief is not inconsistent with the Christian
faith'. A companion to Abbott's popular previous work *The Evolution of
Christianity* (also reissued in the Cambridge Library Collection), this text
presents an innovative and often elegant reconciliation of the ongoing debate
concerning scientific empiricism and Christian belief.

T0372720

Cambridge University Press has long been a pioneer in the reissuing of out-of-print titles from its own backlist, producing digital reprints of books that are still sought after by scholars and students but could not be reprinted economically using traditional technology. The Cambridge Library Collection extends this activity to a wider range of books which are still of importance to researchers and professionals, either for the source material they contain, or as landmarks in the history of their academic discipline.

Drawing from the world-renowned collections in the Cambridge University Library and other partner libraries, and guided by the advice of experts in each subject area, Cambridge University Press is using state-of-the-art scanning machines in its own Printing House to capture the content of each book selected for inclusion. The files are processed to give a consistently clear, crisp image, and the books finished to the high quality standard for which the Press is recognised around the world. The latest print-on-demand technology ensures that the books will remain available indefinitely, and that orders for single or multiple copies can quickly be supplied.

The Cambridge Library Collection brings back to life books of enduring scholarly value (including out-of-copyright works originally issued by other publishers) across a wide range of disciplines in the humanities and social sciences and in science and technology.

The Theology
of an Evolutionist

LYMAN ABBOTT

CAMBRIDGE
UNIVERSITY PRESS

CAMBRIDGE
UNIVERSITY PRESS

University Printing House, Cambridge, CB2 8BS, United Kingdom

Published in the United States of America by Cambridge University Press, New York

Cambridge University Press is part of the University of Cambridge.
It furthers the University's mission by disseminating knowledge in the pursuit of
education, learning and research at the highest international levels of excellence.

www.cambridge.org
Information on this title: www.cambridge.org/9781108001304

This edition first published 1897
This digitally printed version 2013

ISBN 978-1-108-00130-4 Paperback

THE THEOLOGY
OF AN EVOLUTIONIST

BY

LYMAN ABBOTT

LONDON
JAMES CLARKE & CO.
13 & 14 FLEET STREET

The Riverside Press, Cambridge, Mass., U. S. A.
Printed by H. O. Houghton and Company.

PREFACE

THIS book is a companion to two books, similar in character, already published : "The Evolution of Christianity" and "Christianity and Social Problems." Each of these volumes assumes the truth of the principle of evolution as defined by Professor Le Conte,[1] and attempts to apply that principle; the first volume in tracing the history of Christianity as a spiritual force; the second in exhibiting Christianity as a social development; the present one in a statement of Christianity as a system of doctrine. They will, I hope, eventually be followed by a fourth volume, in which the same principle will be applied in an attempt to trace the growth of the Old Testament, and possibly by a fifth, similarly tracing the growth of

---

[1] "A continuous progressive change, according to certain laws, and by means of resident forces." — *Evolution and its Relations to Religious Thought.*

the New Testament, as a body of literature. Neither of them would be complete without duplicating some of the ideas contained in the other volumes; for Christianity as a spiritual force cannot be dissociated from Christianity as a social order, nor either of these from Christianity as a system of thought, embodied in a religious literature. Nevertheless, though they assume the same principle and endeavor to apply it to the same great theme, — the elucidation of the Christian religion, — that theme is so large, and includes such different aspects of life and thought, that I believe it may be truly said that no one of these volumes duplicates its companions.

Each of them has grown out of a previous series of lectures or sermons: the first out of a course of lectures given before the Lowell Institute in Boston; the second out of a course of lectures given before the Meadville Theological Seminary, and subsequently repeated in a modified form in Plymouth Church; the third out of a series of sermons preached in the latter place. But neither volume is a republication of such addresses. Each has been

rewritten for permanent publication, though in
the rewriting free use has been made of the
material employed in the extemporaneous addresses in the pulpit and on the platform.

I received not long ago a letter from a
stranger containing this significant sentence : —

"Forty years ago, while a student at the University
of Munich, one of our professors, Baron Justus von
Liebig, told us, a small circle of students taking extra
lectures in toxicology, in a pause when an animated
controversy about the bottom cause of life sprang
up : . . . 'Gentlemen, if the universe and our planet
ever came to be governed by a wisdom, science, and
penetration on a plan no higher than we mortals are
capable of understanding and mastering, then I would
most fervently wish to be out of it and in a safer
place.'"

With that sentence I heartily concur. If I
could conceive it possible that this universe
were governed by a wisdom no greater than I
am able to comprehend, I should not be able to
believe in a God of infinite wisdom; for finite
wisdom cannot comprehend infinite wisdom. It
is, therefore, no part of my desire, still less of
my purpose, to furnish in this book a system

of scientific or philosophical knowledge which shall explain the mysteries of the universe. It is no part of the desire of evolutionists to furnish such an explanation. Indeed, it would be difficult to find anywhere a nobler statement of the profound mystery of life than is to be found in the writings of Darwin, Huxley, and Herbert Spencer. The very word "agnostic," which has been applied by these gentlemen to themselves, and which was, indeed, first employed by Huxley, is an indication of their frank recognition that the universe cannot be comprehended by finite man. The creed of the evolutionist is all embodied in the statement that life is a growth. But growth is itself a mystery ; and the statement that the universe is full of mysteries is not inconsistent with the statement that the history of the universe is a history of growth.

This volume is not, then, offered as a complete or comprehensive treatment of theological problems. It does not profess to furnish any final solution of the themes of which it treats. It endeavors only to indicate the direction in which modern thought is looking and ought to

look for the interpretation of spiritual life. It
does not profess to add anything to Christian
scholarship, but only to indicate how that material which is the common possession of all
Christian scholars is to be correlated and interpreted. Its sole and simple aim is so to apply
the fundamental principle of evolution to the
problems of religious life and thought, that
the light which that principle has afforded and
the inspiration which it has furnished in the
realm of natural science may be made available
in the spiritual realm to the non-scholastic and
non-professional reader.

LYMAN ABBOTT.

BROOKLYN, N. Y., *September,* 1897.

CONTENTS

AN EVOLUTIONIST'S THEOLOGY

CHAPTER I

SOME DEFINITIONS

THAT the reader and the writer of this volume may understand each other, it is important to begin with some clear definitions. This is the more important because the terms employed are customarily used with widely different meanings. In order to understand the relation of religion, theology, and evolution, we must first understand what we mean by the terms religion, theology, and evolution.

Religion is the life of God in the soul of man. Belief in the reality of religion involves belief that God is, and that He stands in some personal relation to man. But it is not an opinion respecting God, nor an opinion respecting His influence in the world of men. It is a personal consciousness of God. It is a human experience, but an experience of relationship with One who transcends humanity. The creed is

not religion; the creed is a statement of what
certain men think about religion. Worship is
not religion; worship is a method of expressing
religion. The church is not religion; the church
is an organization of men and women, formed
for the purpose of promoting religion. Religion
precedes creeds, worship, church; that is, the life
precedes men's thoughts about the life, men's
expression of the life, men's organizations formed
to promote the life. Religion may be personal
or social; that is, it may be the consciousness of
God in the individual soul, or it may be the con-
current consciousness of God in a great number
of individuals, producing a social or communal
life. In either case it is a life, not an opinion
about life. It is not a definition of God, it is
fellowship with Him; not a definition of sin, but
sorrow because of sin; not a definition of forgiveness, but relief from remorse; not a definition
of redemption, but a new and divine life.

Theology is the science of religion. It is the
result of an attempt made by men to state in an
orderly and systematic manner the facts respecting the life of God in the soul of man. It involves intellectual definition of the various forms
of consciousness which constitute the religious
life. Its relation to religion is the relation of
other sciences to the vital phenomena which they
endeavor to explain. With the growth of the

human intellect there comes a wiser study of life, a better understanding of it, a new definition of its terms, and a new classification of its phenomena. The life does not change, but man's understanding of it changes. There is a new astronomy, though the stars are old; a new botany, though vegetable life is unchanged; a new chemistry, though the constituent elements of the universe are the same. So there is a new theology, though not a new religion. God, sin, repentance, forgiveness, love, remain essentially unchanged, but the definitions of God, sin, repentance, forgiveness, and love are changed from generation to generation. There is as little danger of undermining religion by new definitions of theology as there is of blotting out the stars from the heavens by a new astronomy. But as religion is the life of God in the soul of man, definitions which give to man a clearer and a more intelligible understanding of that life will promote it, and definitions which are, or seem to be, irrational, will tend to impede or impair it. To this extent theology affects the religious life as other sciences do not affect the life with which they have to deal.

Evolution is described by John Fiske as "God's way of doing things." Theology also may be described as an attempt to explain God's way of doing things. Thus, to a certain extent the science of evolution and the science of theology have the same ultimate end. Both attempt to furnish an orderly, rational, and self-consistent account of phenomena. The supposed inconsistency between science and religion is really an inconsistency between two sciences. The theologian and the scientist have given different, and to some extent inconsistent, accounts of God's way of doing things. It is important for us to know which account is correct. It is even religiously desirable that we should know, since our understanding of God's influence upon the human soul affects that influence.

The current theology is Roman in its origin. It assumes as an axiom a God apart from the universe and ruling over it, as the Roman Emperor was apart from the Roman Empire and ruled over it. It conceives of His government as a series of successive interventions. He creates the world out of nothing in the space of six days, and then rests. Man sins, and lest he should become immortal and so independent of his sin, God intervenes and drives him from the garden. His sin grows greater; God intervenes again, sweeps the human race from the globe, and makes a new beginning. Man has no natural capacity to know God. God compassionately intervenes once more, and makes to man special revelations; outside the race to which these revelations are

made there is no possibility of the knowledge of
God, — that is, no possibility of true religion.
To attest this revelation which God has made
of Himself, interventions in the laws of nature
which He has ordained are necessary. These
interventions, called miracles, are essential to
revelation, and revelation is essential to the
knowledge of God, — that is, to true religion.
Thus theology assumes that God's way of doing
things in the material world is the way of a
mechanic operating upon a machine; His way
of doing things in the spiritual world is the way
of a king ruling over an empire. God is some
one outside of nature and outside of men, operating upon nature and upon men.

This conception of the universe as set in
operation by a Great First Cause, but operated
continuously by secondary causes, occasionally
modified in their action by the original Creator,
is one which I formerly entertained, and there is
no inherent inconsistency or irrationality in it.
It is certainly quite consonant with faith in a living God, in revelation, in incarnation, in atonement, in immortality. But it is rejected to-day
by the great mass of scientific thinkers, and by
an increasing number of philosophical thinkers.
They have seen more and more reason to believe
that all forces are one force, and that events
formerly attributed to interventions of an appar-

ently arbitrary will are really due to the operation of this one force. They have seen one supposed intervention after another eliminated, and
they have come to believe that when the universe
is fully understood it will appear that there are
no such interventions. We are all agreed that
there are fewer than our ancestors thought there
were; the scientist of to-day thinks it probable
that there are none. It is not my object to
show that the scientist is right, but to show that,
if he is right, he may still hold to spiritual faith
in God, Bible, Christ, Sacrifice. This volume
is addressed not to disbelievers in evolution to
prove that they are mistaken, but to believers
in evolution to show them that their belief is not
inconsistent with the Christian faith; it is inconsistent with much in the old *theology*, but
not with anything in the old *faith*.

It is true that I am an evolutionist, and inclined to be a radical evolutionist. It is perhaps proper to indicate in a paragraph the
reasons for my change of opinion, — a change
which has taken place gradually and almost un-
consciously.

In the first place, all biologists are evolutionists, probably without a single exception. They
are not all Darwinians, — that is, they do not
all regard " struggle for existence and survival
of the fittest " as an adequate statement of the

process of evolution. Indeed, it may be said that this is no longer by any one regarded as a complete summary of the process, even if it were so regarded by Darwin himself, which is doubtful. I am not an expert biologist; few ministers are. We are not competent to pass any independent judgment of value on the question, What is the process of life in its earlier forms? We have not the scientific habit of mind which enables us to sift the evidence and reach a conclusion. How many of those who read this chapter could pass a creditable examination on the question at issue between the Ptolemaic and the Copernican theories of astronomy, or the atomic and undulatory theory of light? Probably but few. We accept the testimony of the experts when they have reached a conclusion. This is my first reason for being an evolutionist. Practically all scientists, I believe absolutely all biologists, are evolutionists. They have proved themselves careful, painstaking, assiduous students of life. I assume the correctness of their conclusion. I have studied, it is true, the writings of Darwin, Huxley, Haeckel, Tyndall, and the later epitomes of Le Conte, Drummond, and Tyler, and have read the more important of the criticisms on the other side, — enough to see that the hypothesis of evolution has a groundwork of fact and reason. But I accept evolution, as

a statement of the process of physical life, not
from a personal scientific investigation, which I
have not the training to conduct, but upon the
substantially unanimous testimony of those who
have such training.

On the other hand, the minister ought to be
a special student of the moral life. He ought
to know man as a moral actor, literature as the
expression of his moral consciousness, history as
the record of his moral progress, society as a
moral organism. He ought to be able to pass
something approximating an expert judgment
on the question whether and how far evolution
explains "the history of the process" by which
the individual man, his literature, his history,
his social and political organisms, have come to
be what they are. To this subject I have given
years of study, sometimes systematic, sometimes
desultory, sometimes in theoretical investigations, sometimes in practical applications. The
result of this study has been a conclusion, very
gradually formed, that the history of that process
is best expressed by the word "evolution," —
that is, that the process has been one of continuous progressive growth, from a lower to a higher,
from a simpler to a more complex organization,
under the influence of resident forces, and in
accordance with law. And this opinion has
been confirmed by Bible study. It appears to

me to harmonize better with the general spirit of Biblical teaching than does the anti-evolutionary conception of life. These two reasons, the substantially unanimous judgment of experts in a department with which I am not familiar, and my own independent judgment in a department with which I have some familiarity, have led me to accept evolution as a history of the process of life, or as " God's way of doing things."

I acknowledge myself, then, a radical evolutionist, — it is hardly necessary to say a theistic evolutionist. I reverently and heartily accept the axiom of theology that a personal God is the foundation of all life; but I also believe that God has but one way of doing things ; that His way may be described in one word as the way of growth, or development, or evolution, terms which are substantially synonymous ; that He resides in the world of nature and in the world of men ; that there are no laws of nature which are not the laws of God's own being ; that there are no forces of nature, that there is only one divine, infinite force, always proceeding from, always subject to the will of God ; that there are not occasional or exceptional theophanies, but that all nature and all life is one great theophany ; that there are not occasional interventions in the order of life which bear witness to the presence of God, but that life is itself a perpetual witness to His presence ; that He transcends all phenomena, and yet is the creative, controlling, directing force in all phenomena. In so far as the theologian and the evolutionist differ in their interpretation of the history of life — that is, upon the question whether God's way of doing things is a way of successive interventions or a continuous and unbroken progress — I agree with the evolutionist, not with the theologian. My object in this volume is to show that religion — that is, the life of God in the soul of man — is better comprehended, and will better be promoted, by the philosophy which regards all life as divine, and God's way of doing things as the way of a continuous, progressive change, according to certain laws and by means of one resident force, than by the philosophy which supposes that some things are done by natural forces and according to natural laws, and others by special interventions of a Divine Will, acting from without, for the purpose of correcting errors or filling gaps.

The affirmation that all growth is due to " resident forces," or a " resident force," requires, perhaps, some additional explanation, for it is to this affirmation that the critics of evolution chiefly object. They generally agree that the interventions from without are fewer than we used to think; but they still believe that there must be or have been some interventions: as in the passage from the inorganic to the organic, and again from the vegetable to the animal, and yet again from the animal to the human. "That phrase," says Professor W. Douglass MacKenzie in the "Bibliotheca Sacra,"[1] "'by means of resident forces,' is one to which exception of the most serious kind must be taken. . . . In that definition of evolution no man of science would understand by the phrase 'by means of resident forces,' this, that God is continually pouring the energies of his Divine will into created forms, and carrying them forward to their further development. Any man of science would understand that definition to mean, that the evolution of any form of life takes place wholly by means of the forces already resident in the forms of existence which had been realized in the preceding stages of history." I think that as matter of literary interpretation Dr. MacKenzie is mistaken, and that Professor Le Conte and Professor Drummond, both of them men of science, do clearly understand substantially what Dr. MacKenzie says no man of science would understand by the phrase "resident forces," and that even Professor Tyndall implies that understanding as a probable opinion, though not as a

[1] *Bibliotheca Sacra*, July, 1897: "Evolution and Christian Doctrine."

positive faith. The theology and the science of
the past have agreed in assuming what I think
the theology and the science of the future will
agree in denying, that God sits apart from
nature, and that there are natural forces and
natural laws which operate independently of
Him. Starting from this assumption, of course
theology has resisted bitterly every attempt to
lessen the number of interventions in the order
of nature, because the inevitable result was to
lessen the evidence of a Divine presence in the
world. Nevertheless, both the religious and the
scientific world have come to believe in a greatly
lessened number of interventions, until now science has reached with practical unanimity these
three conclusions : first, there is but one force,
manifesting itself in different forms; second,
that this force is never increased or diminished
in amount, only varied in form ; and third, that
this force, if we believe it to be directed to intelligent ends, is sufficient to account for all the
phenomena of nature and life, so that there is
no reason to believe in any interventions from
without. I believe that the theology of the
future will frankly and gladly accept these conclusions, instead of resisting them and endeavoring to discover some evidences of interventions
constantly lessening in number if not in magni-
tude. It, too, will affirm that there is only one

force, the "Infinite and Eternal Energy from which all things proceed." It will affirm that this Infinite and Eternal Energy is never increased or diminished; that, in other words, God, who varies infinitely in His manifestations, varies in no whit in His real life. It will affirm that there are and can be no interventions in this resident force, this Infinite and Eternal Energy, for if there were there would be a second God, superior to the God who resides in the universe and controlling Him. And finally, it will affirm that this Infinite and Eternal Energy is itself intelligent and beneficent, — an infinitely wise and holy Spirit, dwelling within the universe and shaping it from within, much as the human spirit dwells within the human body and forms and controls it from within. Scientifically this is the affirmation that the forces of nature are one vital force; theologically it is the affirmation that God is an Immanent God. " Resident forces " and " Divine Immanence " are different forms of the same statement. According to this view, it is not correct to say that " God, the one Force, did somehow bring into being the earliest forms of matter with resident forces." [1] It is correct to say that from the earliest time we know anything about, God, the one Resident Force, has been shaping matter

[1] Dr. W. D. MacKenzie. *Bibliotheca Sacra*, July, 1897.

into its various forms. It is not correct to say
that " the interactions of the various portions of
this primeval matter did, by continuous and
progressive changes, result in the production of
all later forms of existence, including life and
consciousness, reason and conscience." [1] It is
correct to say that all later forms of existence,
including life and consciousness, reason and
conscience, are the manifestations of His power,
and the revelations of His presence who is God,
" the all in all." [2] Nor is this inconsistent with
the belief that the heaven of heavens cannot
contain Him. The Divine Spirit which resides
in Nature transcends Nature, as the human
spirit which resides in the body transcends the
body. The Divine Spirit which is manifested
in all phenomena is more than the sum of all
phenomena, as the human spirit which is manifested in all the activities of a life is more than
the sum of those activities. The belief that the
Divine Spirit resides *in* the universe is no more
pantheism than belief that the human spirit
resides *in* the body is materialism. This faith
in the Divine Immanence, in an Intelligent and
Beneficent Will working in the so-called forces
of Nature, is neither atheistic nor pantheistic.
Belief that all energies are vital is not belief

---

[1] Dr. W. D. MacKenzie. *Bibliotheca Sacra*, July, 1897.
[2] τὰ πάντα ἐν πᾶσιν. 1 Corinthians xv. 28.

that there are no vital energies. Belief that all
resident forces are Divine is not belief that
there is no true Divinity.

It seemed necessary to make this explanation
to guard, if possible, against the common misapprehension of the evolutionist's position, as that
of one whose faith in "resident forces" implies
no faith in God. The theistic evolutionist believes that God is the one Resident Force, that
He is in His world; that His method of work in
His world is the method of growth; and that
the history of the world, whether it be the history of creation, of providence, or of redemption, whether the history of redemption in the
race or of redemption in the individual soul, is
the history of a growth in accordance with the
great law interpreted and uttered in that one
word evolution.

CHAPTER II

WHEN man would make a rose with tools, he fashions petals and leaves of wax, colors them, manufactures a stalk by the same mechanical process, — and the rose is done. When God makes a rose, he lets a bird or a puff of wind drop a seed into the ground; out of the seed there emerges a stalk; and out of the stalk, branches; and on these branches, buds; and out of these buds roses unfold; and the rose is never done, for it goes on endlessly repeating itself. This is the difference between manufacture and growth. Man's method is the method of manufacture; God's method is the method of growth. What man makes is a finished product, — death. What God makes is an always finishing and never finished product, — life. What man makes has no reproductive power within itself. What God makes goes on reproducing itself, with ever new forms and in ever new vitality. The doctrine of evolution, in its radical form, is the doctrine that all God's processes are processes of growth, — not processes of manufacture.

Evolution is the history of a process, not the explanation of a cause. The doctrine of evolution is an attempt on the part of scientific men to state what is the process of life; not an attempt to state what is the cause of life. When Isaac Newton discovered and announced the doctrine of attraction and gravitation, he did not undertake to explain why the apple falls from the bough to the earth, nor why the earth revolves around the sun in its orbit; he simply stated what he had seen, — that all matter acts as if its bodies were attracted to one another inversely as the square of the distance. So the evolutionist does not attempt to explain the cause of phenomena; he simply recites their history.

A correspondent recently wrote me a letter saying in substance, " I am sorry that you have taken up with that dangerous doctrine of evolution. Huxley and Darwin and Tyndall tell us that matter somehow or other once upon a time began to create itself." He is mistaken. He would find it difficult to point to page or paragraph in any scientific writer as authority for any such notion of evolution. Evolution does not undertake to give the cause of phenomena at all; it simply recites their processes. A

man may be an atheistic evolutionist — that
is, he may believe that there is no intelligent
cause lying back of phenomena. Haeckel is an
atheistic evolutionist. Or he may be a theistic evolutionist, — that is, he may believe that
the cause lying back of all phenomena is a
divine, intelligent, loving Person ; Dr. McCosh
of Princeton was a theistic evolutionist. The
evolutionist is simply one who understands the
history of life to be a history of growth. " Evolution," says Mr. Huxley, " or development, is
at present employed in biology as a general
name for the history of the steps by which any
living being has acquired the morphological and
physiological characters which distinguish it ; "
and on that Mr. Henry Drummond, an eminent
evolutionist, comments as follows : —

" Evolution is simply history, a history of
steps, a general name for the history of the steps
by which the world has come to what it is.
According to this general definition, the story of
evolution is narrative.   It may be wrongly told ;
it may be colored, exaggerated, over or under
stated, like the record of any other set of facts ;
it may be told with a theological bias, or with
an anti-theological bias ; theories of the process
may be added by this thinker or by that, but
these are not of the substance of the story.
Whether history is told by a Gibbon or a Green,

the facts remain ; and whether evolution be told
by a Haeckel or a Wallace, we accept the narrative so far as it is a rendering of nature, and
no more. It is true, before this story can be
fully told, centuries still must pass. At present
there is not a chapter of the record that is
wholly finished. The manuscript is already
worn with erasures, the writing is often blurred,
the very language is uncouth and strange. Yet
even now the outline of a continuous story is
beginning to appear, — a story whose chief cre-
dential lies in the fact that no imagination of
man could have designed a spectacle so wonderful, or worked out a plot at once so intricate
and so transcendently simple."

Evolution, then, — let us understand this at
the outset, — is the history of a process, not the
explanation of a cause. The evolutionist believes that God's processes are the processes of
growth, not of manufacture.

We are all partial evolutionists. Every man
believes that to a large extent the divine processes are processes of growth. He believes that
the rose grows from a seed or a cutting ; that all
the vegetable matter in the world has come to its
present condition by growth from earlier forms.
He believes that this principle of growth applies
to the animal as well as to the vegetable kingdom. He believes that every horse was once a

colt, and every man was once a babe. He believes, too, in growth as a principle of history:
that the American nation has grown from colonial to national greatness; that literature has
grown from primitive to sublime forms. He
thus believes that most of the processes of God
are processes of growth.

The radical evolutionist believes that all divine
processes, so far as we are able to understand
them, are processes of growth; that as God
makes the oak out of the acorn, and the rose out
of the cutting, and the man out of the babe, and
the nation out of the colony, and the literature
out of the alphabet, so God has made all things
by the development of higher from lower forms.
He believes that, so far as he can see, God is
never a manufacturer, but always does His work
by growth processes. The best simple definition
of this process that I have ever seen is Le
Conte's: "Evolution is continuous progressive
change, according to certain laws and by means
of resident forces."

It is, first, continuous progressive change.
The rose the man makes does not go through continuous progressive change. He makes a little
to-day, leaves it, begins again to-morrow, leaves
it a year, comes back next year. He finds that
he is making it wrong, changes his mind, makes
it over again. There is no necessary continuity

in his work. The work that man does is not
done according to certain laws. It is often arbitrary. He makes the rose in one way to-day,
in another way to-morrow, simply because the
notion so takes him. His work is done by force
external to the thing that is made ; not by force
operating from within, but by force applied from
without. God's work, on the contrary, we evolutionists believe, is the work of progressive
change, — a change from a lower to a higher
condition ;[1] from a simpler to a more complex
condition. It is a change wrought according to
certain laws which are capable of study. It is
never arbitrary. Finally, this process of growth
is produced by forces that lie within the phenomena themselves. The tools that God uses
are in the structure that is being formed, or in
its environment. The force that makes the rose
what it is inheres in the plant, in the soil, in the
sunlight. God dwells in nature, fashioning it
according to His will by vital processes from
within, not by mechanical processes from without. The former theory of creation was of creation by manufacture. It was that God said to
himself one day, six, eight, or ten thousand
years ago, " I will make a world ; " that He proceeded to make it, in six successive days ; and that

[1] This is the object of evolution, though incidental to it are
other results, such as moral development or degeneracy.

when six days were over the world was finished. As science disclosed the history of the past, men changed their conception of the creative days to longer and yet longer epochs. But still the conception of manufacture lingered in the thought of the Church. Some of the old mediæval writers undertook even to state what time of the year the world was made; one of them, I believe, argues that it must have been in the autumn, because apples were ripe. Still many persons conceive of creation as a process of manufacture, and of God as a kind of architect or masterbuilder, laying foundations, putting up pillars, carving, upholstering, decorating, — constructing the edifice in carpenter fashion.

Over against this conception of creation by manufacture, we are coming to accept the conception of creation by evolution. It would require one far more familiar with scientific detail than I am to give the process with scientific accuracy; but it is possible to indicate the broad outlines, and I am facilitated in doing this by a somewhat vague recollection of an experiment which I saw performed by Dr. R. Ogden Doremus many years ago. On the platform where the chemist was performing his experiments was a great glass box, and in that box a colorless liquid, into which he poured a colored liquid, — red, if my memory serves me right; and running through this box, with little arms extending from it, was a cylinder, with a crank at the top. While we sat there this colored material gathered itself together in a gobular form before our eyes. It was of precisely the same specific density as the colorless liquid in which it had been plunged, so that there was no attraction of gravitation to carry it to the bottom. Then gradually, very slowly at first, the lecturer began a movement with this crank, and the globe, following the cylinder which he revolved, began revolving itself very slowly, and gradually more and more rapidly, and, as it revolved, flattened at the poles, and presently, as the cylinder became more and more rapid, flung out from itself, I forget now whether a ring or a single globe.[1]

---

[1] Dr. Doremus has kindly furnished me with the following accurate account of this most interesting illustration of the process of " Creation by Evolution." It is an illustration which amounts to demonstration to any one who has ever seen it. Olive oil (colored red that it might be better seen) was poured on water. It floated on the *denser* liquid. Another portion of the oil was poured in alcohol. It sank in this *lighter* liquid.

A third portion of the oil was poured into a carefully prepared mixture of water and alcohol, having exactly the same specific gravity as the oil. The oil assumed the shape of a perfect sphere. The earth is round, the sun, moon, and planets are round, every star that decorates the heavens is round; hence they were once liquid, or are now fluid.

A glass axis inserted through the centre of the sphere of oil was slowly revolved. The globe flattened at its poles and dilated at its equator. Our earth has this shape. The

So we saw, before our eyes, the nebular
hypothesis illustrated. In some far-off epoch,

globe of oil was revolved *more* rapidly. It then flattened to
a greater extent, or was more oblate, like the planet Jupiter,
when the difference between its polar and equatorial diameters
is 5000 miles. Its oblateness can be seen with a powerful
telescope.

Our earth revolves at its equator at the rate of 1000 mile,
per hour, Jupiter over 26,000 miles per hour. Jupiter has the
density of water, while our earth is five times as dense; —
these two causes account for the difference in figures or shapes
of these planets.

On turning the oil globe more rapidly, it formed a ring like
the rings of Saturn. When the speed of revolution was still
more increased the ring broke into many spheres, some large,
others small; each of these revolved on its axis, around the
common centre. The sun turns from west to east; Mercury,
nestling closest to our peerless parent, turns from west to east
on its axis and around the central sun; so also Venus, the
Earth, Mars, the small planets beween Mars and Jupiter (over
200 in number), Jupiter, Saturn, Uranus, and the remotest,
Neptune, all revolve in this same direction, and in the same
plane. According to Herschel, Struve, Argelander, and other
astronomers, our sun with his princely retinue of planets,
satellites and fiery comets is flying through space towards the
star π in the constellation Hercules, with the velocity of half
a million miles per diem. Maedler has proved that our
whole galaxy of stars is revolving in a mighty circle, the
star Alcyone, of the Pleiades, being nearest the central point.
" Canst thou bind the sweet influences of Pleiades ? " (Job
xxxviii. 31.) Eighteen million two hundred thousand years
must elapse to complete one revolution around this distant
centre. In this grand circular movement are minor rotations
(like eddies in a stream of water) of double, triple, and multiple stars, joining in the mazy celestial dance.

Dr. Lee, of the Lowell Observatory, while in Mexico dis-

misty matter hung nebulous in the universe.
It came together as a globe under the law of attraction of gravitation. It began its revolution,
set in motion by that infinite and eternal energy
which is an infinite and eternal mystery, and
which I believe is God. As it revolved, by the
very process of revolution it flattened at the
poles. As it revolved it cooled, the mist turned
to water, the water to solid. From this revolving globe a ring, like the ring of Saturn,
was flung off, and the revolving ring itself was
broken by the very process of revolution into
separate luminaries. So grew the moons, so the
planetary system. In this globe was, as still
there is, life, — that is, an infinite and eternal
energy which is an infinite and eternal mystery,
that is, God. Out of this life, manifesting this
God, grew, as the rose grows from its seed, the
lower forms, and, by successive processes from
these lower forms, other higher forms, and

covered, since the 1st of last January, 300,000 double and
triple stars in the southern heavens. Thousands of other
stellar universes revolve in a manner similar to our own galaxy of suns. Some of the nebulæ have the shape of a ring,
others are oval (because of being seen at an angle). Some
have a dumb-bell shape, which can be imitated by revolving the oil-globe in the mixture of alcohol and water, when
the axis is not exactly in the centre of the oil-sphere. Herschel asserted that some of the nebulæ are so remote that
their light (with its velocity of over 186,000 miles per second)
has been 3,000,000 of years in reaching our eyes.

from these forms others still higher, until at last the world came to be what it is to-day. There never was a time when the world was done. It is not done to-day. It is in the making. In the belief of the evolutionists, the same processes that were going on in the creative days are going on here and now. Still the nebulæ are gathering together in globes; still globes are beginning their revolution ; still they are flattening at the poles; still they are cooling and becoming solid; still in them are springing up the forms of life. In our own globe the same forces that were operative in the past to make the world what it is are operative to-day : still from the seeds are springing the plants; still the mountains are being pushed up by volcanic forces below ; still chasms are being made by the earthquake ; all the methods and all the processes that went on in those first great days are still proceeding. Creative days ! Every day is a creative day. Every spring is a creative spring. God is always creating. Such, briefly and imperfectly outlined, is the doctrine of creation by evolution.

Does this doctrine deny, or imply a denial, that there is intelligence in the universe? Is my correspondent right who thinks that Spencer and Huxley and Tyndall imagine that matter makes itself and governs itself? Is it true

that the evolutionist believes, or if he be logical
must believe, that there is no intelligence that
plans, no wisdom that directs? Paley's famous
illustration suggests that a man going along
the road finds a watch; picks it up; examines
it; sees that it will keep time; knows that
there was some intelligence that devised this
watch. Suppose this watch which he picks up
and puts into his pocket, after he has carried
it for a year, produces another watch that will
keep time; does that show less intelligence, or
more? Suppose this watch which he picks up
and carries in his pocket drops from itself in
a year's time a little egg, and out of that egg
there comes a perfect watch a year later; does
that show less intelligence, or more? Is the
natural rose, with all its forces within itself,
less wonderful than the artificial rose, which the
man makes in imitation of it out of wax? The
processes of growth are infinitely more wonderful than the processes of manufacture. It
is easier by far to comprehend the intelligence
that makes the cuckoo which springs from the
cuckoo clock to note the time, than to comprehend the intelligence that makes the living bird
which springs from his nest and sings his song
to the morning sun. Growth is more wonderful than manufacture. Growth has in it more
evidence of marvelous intelligence than any

manufacture. " In that statement appears the
clergyman," says the critic.   No ! The statement is Professor Huxley's : —

"The student of Nature wonders the more
and is astonished the less, the more conversant
he becomes with her operations ; but of all the
perennial miracles she offers to his inspection,
perhaps the most worthy of admiration is the
development of a plant or of an animal from its
embryo. Examine the recently laid egg of some
common animal, such as a salamander or a newt.
Is it a minute spheroid in which the best microscope will reveal nothing but a structureless sac,
inclosing a glairy fluid, holding granules in sus-
pension.   But strange possibilities lie dormant
in that semi-fluid globule.   Let a moderate sup-
ply of warmth reach its watery cradle, and the
plastic matter undergoes changes so rapid, and
yet so steady and purpose-like in their succession,
that one can only compare them to those operated by a skilled modeler upon a formless lump
of clay.   As with an invisible trowel, the mass
is divided and subdivided into smaller and
smaller portions, until it is reduced to an aggre-
gation of granules not too large to build withal
the finest fabrics of the nascent organism.   And
then, it is as if a delicate finger traced out the
line to be occupied by the spinal column, and
moulded the contour of the body ; pinching up

the head at one end, the tail at the other, and fashioning flank and limb into due salamandrine proportions in so artistic a way that, after watching the process hour by hour, one is almost involuntarily possessed by the notion that some, more subtle aid to vision than an achromatic would show the hidden artist, with his plan before him, striving with skillful manipulation to perfect his work."

That is the account of an evolutionary process by an evolutionist who certainly will not be accused of theological prepossessions.

Does this doctrine of creation by evolution take God away from the world? It seems to me that it brings Him a great deal nearer. The Hindu believed that God was too great to stoop to the making of the world, so He hatched out an egg from which issued a number of little gods, and the little gods made the world. Something like that has been our past philosophy. A great First Cause in the remote past set secondary causes at work, and we stand only in the presence of secondary causes. But Herbert Spencer, the typical agnostic evolutionist, affirms that we are ever *in the presence* of an Infinite and Eternal Energy from which all things proceed. True, Herbert Spencer says that He is the Unknown; but the theist who believes with Matthew Arnold that this Infinite and Eternal Energy is an energy that makes for righteousness in human history, and the Christian theist who believes that this Infinite and Eternal Energy has manifested Himself in Jesus Christ, and has purpose and will and love and intelligence, believes no less certainly than Herbert Spencer that we are ever in His presence. There is no chasm of six thousand years between the evolutionist and his Creator. The evolutionist lives in the creative days and sees the creative processes taking place before him.

CHAPTER III

THE GENESIS OF SIN

THE problem of sin is not to be confounded with the fact of sin. As to the fact, there is no room for question. All the great dramatists have recognized it in their portrayal of remorse, indignation, penalty, repentance, forgiveness, restoration. The great historians have recognized it, in depicting the struggle of righteousness with moral evil. Religious worship is largely founded upon it; for religious worship is largely an endeavor of the worshiper to rid himself of the present burden and the future penalty of sin. All government recognizes it; for certainly the first if not also the chief function of government is to protect the innocent from the sins of the sinful. He who denies the fact of sin denies the police and the prison, the temple and the priest, the battle-field and the martyrdom, Shakespeare and Æschylus. The problem is not, Is there sin? but, Whence comes it? If we are to cure a disease, we must know its nature and origin. What is the nature and

origin of sin, the cure of which is alike the problem of government, education, and religion, —
of the courts, the school, and the church ?

To this question there are two answers, — the
theological and the evolutionary. The theological is that God created man perfect, that man
fell by voluntary transgression of the law which
God imposed upon him, and that in consequence
of that fall sin entered the world and poisoned
the entire race, in one of three ways, — for on
this point theologians are not agreed : either because the whole race was *in* Adam as the oak is
in the acorn, and sinned with him ; or because
the whole race was represented by Adam and
is held responsible for his act, much as a nation
is held responsible for the acts of its representa-
tives ; or because the whole race descended from
Adam and inherited, by the law of heredity, his
sinful nature from him.

The evolutionary answer to this question,
What is Sin ? it is the object of this chapter to
give.

Man is an animal, — about that there can be
no question, — a vertebrate animal, belonging to
the class mammal, and by most scientists reck-
oned in the family of apes. And he has ascended
from a lower animal. Whether the whole human race has so ascended is not absolutely certain, — the so-called missing link has not been

discovered; the fossil man is far removed from
the highest ape. But, wherever the race came
from as a race, there is absolutely no question
that every individual of the race has passed
through animal stages in reaching manhood.
Embryology has established beyond all question,
so far as accurate, scientific, microscopic examination can establish anything, that all animals
begin in germs so absolutely alike that the
finest microscope can detect no difference, and
in proceeding from this germ each individual
passes through successive stages of animal life.
Whether the race did or not, each individual
man does. He originates in a form nowise different from that of lower animals, depends upon
the same contrivances for his nutrition and development in the earlier stages of his existence,
passes through the successive forms of lower orders, is at one period of his existence in nowise
distinguishable from the earlier form of the dog,
a little later does not differ from that of the ape,
and so proceeds from one state to another until
he is born a human child. When the minister, whose acquaintance with theology is greater
than his acquaintance with science, asserts that
the notion that man has ascended from a lower
order is pure imagination, he speaks without
knowledge. The origin of the race is a matter
of hypothesis; not so the origin of the indivi-

dual. He is known to be derived from a germ indistinguishable from that of the lower animals. The process of his development is seen and known, not imagined.

In speaking upon embryology, I disavow speaking as an expert. I only attempt to interpret to non-expert readers the conclusions of expert observers, my object being, let me repeat, not to demonstrate even the conclusions of embryology, but to state them, so that the non-expert reader may understand a little the ground on which the scientific evolutionist bases his acceptance of evolution as applied to the development of man. To illustrate this conclusion of embryology a little more fully, I quote substantially, though with condensations, from the volume "Darwin and After Darwin," by George John Romanes, taking this volume simply because it is a convenient epitome and is in the main untechnical in its statements.

All life begins with a germ-cell. "If the theory of evolution is true, what should we expect to happen when these germ-cells are fertilized and so enter upon their severally distinct processes of development? Assuredly we should expect to find that the higher organisms passed through the same phases of development as the lower organisms, up to the time when their higher characters begin to become apparent.

. . . And this is just what we do find. Take, for example, the case of the highest organism, man. Like that of all other organisms, unicellular or multicellular, his development starts from the nucleus of a single cell. . . . When his animality becomes established, he exhibits the fundamental anatomical qualities which characterize such lowly animals as polyps and jelly-fish, and even when he is marked off as the vertebrate it cannot be said whether he is to be a fish, a reptile, a bird, or a beast. Later on, it becomes evident that he is to be a mammal; but not till later still can it be said to which order of mammals he belongs." In the chapter on " Embryology " Mr. Romanes traces with illustrations the process through which the individual man passes from this germ to his final completion as an infant man. His illustrations show, side by side, the embryos of a fish, a salamander, a tortoise, a bird, a hog, a calf, a rabbit, and a man, in three successive stages of development. Interpreting these pictures, which speak to the eye, Mr. Romanes truly says : "We can see that there is very little difference between the eight animals at the earliest of the three stages represented, all having fish-like tails, gill-slits, and so on. In the next stage further differentiation has taken place, but it will be observed that the limbs are still so rudimentary that even in the case of the man they are considerably shorter than the tail; but in the third stage the distinctive characters are well marked." In the light of these facts, the evolutionist cannot doubt that the individual man ascended from a lower animal condition; that growth, or development, is God's way of creating the individual man; and he not unnaturally concludes that it is probable that the whole race similarly proceeded from a lower animal condition, and that growth or development has been God's way of producing the race.

There are two methods which the Christian teacher may pursue in meeting this conclusion: he may declare that if this conclusion is accepted, the Christian religion is overthrown, because the Christian religion depends upon an acceptance of the scientific accuracy of the first chapter of Genesis; or he may accept the conclusion of the evolutionist as certainly probable, if not absolutely demonstrable, and may attempt to show that the Christian's faith in the reality of sin as an awful fact, and the reality of redemption as a glorious fact, is entirely consistent with the opinion that man has ascended from a lower animal order, and that development or growth is God's way of doing things; and he may maintain that the first chapters of Genesis are not to be regarded as authoritative scientific statements respecting the methods of creation, the origin of the race, or its duration upon the earth. I firmly believe that the former method, which sets theological theories against scientifically ascertained facts, is fatal to the current theology and injurious to the spirit of religion; and that the second method, which frankly recognizes the facts of life, and appreciates the spirit of the scientists, whose patient and assiduous endeavor has brought those facts to light, will commend the spirit of religion to the new generation, and will benefit — not impair — theology as a science, by compelling its reconstruction.

I accept, then, the conclusions of the embryologist: we are animals, we ascended from lower animals. Whether we like the fact or not, it is a fact.

But we are more than animals. We all know that fact also. There is a great gap between manhood and brutehood. It is shown by language, which no brutes use in any perfection approximating that of man. It is shown in tools, which animals do not to any extent employ. It is shown in the largeness of reasoning power, which immeasurably exceeds all reasoning power of animals. It is shown in the apparently illimitable development possible in man, while animal development halts at a clearly marked line. It is shown, above all, in the

moral and spiritual nature of man, — in his independent conscience, in his clear perception of
right and wrong, in his sense of the infinite and
the eternal, in his worship. Practically it may
be said that there is no race of men on the face
of the globe that has not something akin to worship, and no race of animals that has.

Man, then, is an animal, and has ascended
from a lower animal; but he is something immeasurably more than an animal. How did he
get this something more? At what stage in his
existence was it implanted in him? In what
way? On this point the Church has never
agreed. Theologians have been divided in opinion into four schools, giving four separate answers to this question. The first is creationism,
— the doctrine that into every man, at some
stage of his existence, presumptively at the time
of his birth, God, by a miraculous or supernatural act, implants the divine spirit. The second is traducianism, — the doctrine that at some
period in the history of the human race God
breathed the breath of divine life into some remote ancestor, and that the race has inherited
that breath of life throughout all subsequent
ages. The third is evolutionism, — the doctrine
that this higher life of man, this moral, this
ethical, this spiritual nature, has been developed
by natural processes as the higher physical

phases of life have been developed by natural processes. The fourth is conditional immortality, — the doctrine that the spiritual nature is developed and made dominant in men only as by faith they lay hold on God, and that there are men upon the earth who to all intents and purposes are but little higher than the animals, and will sink back into the animal and finally become extinct. Whichever of these views one holds, he may still hold that man is two men. He may think that the divine element is implanted in each individual at birth; or he may think that it was implanted in some individual at a certain point in the race development and has since been inherited by all his posterity; or he may think that it is implanted by a special act of divine grace, not in all individuals, but only in a certain elect circle, — those whom God chooses, or those who choose to accept it; or he may believe that it comes through evolutionary process eventually to all men, growing gradually out of that which is not spiritual; but, whichever theory of its origin he entertains, he may be sure that this spiritual life exists to-day. We have the spiritual life, — the life of conscience, faith, hope, love. On this fact religion is based; it does not depend on the question where this spiritual life came from, or at what point in the development of the race or the individual it

began to appear. For religion has to do with
what is and what is to be. It leaves science to
deal with the past.

The evolutionist, then, no less than the creationist, believes that every man is two men. He
believes that God made man out of the dust of
the earth, — that is, out of a lower order. Yes!
even out of inorganic matter. He believes this
none the less because he thinks he can trace, in
imagination, the process by which during a long
course of ages the preparations were made for
the perfection of the animal man, and because
he knows that he can trace by observation the
process by which the individual animal man is
gradually formed out of a germ indistinguishable from that of other animals. He believes no
less than the creationist that God breathes into
man the breath of a divine life. He believes
this none the less because he thinks he can trace
the process by which reason is developed out of
instinct, and patience out of passivity, and sympathy out of imagining the troubles of others,
and carefulness out of parental instinct, and
conscience out of approbativeness, and honesty
and honor out of self-interest.[1] In short, he
believes that development is a divine process as
firmly as the creationist believes that creation

[1] See Drummond's *Ascent of Man*, chapter viii., and Darwin's *Expression of Emotions in Man and Animals*, passim.

is a divine process, and no less divine because it is gradual.

When this higher life is breathed into man — whether by an instant act or a gradual process is, religiously speaking, a matter of indifference — man comes under the law of the higher life. This law is always sovereign whenever, in the process of evolution, the lower passes into a higher stage of life. When the inorganic is taken up into the plant and made vegetable, it becomes subject to the law of vegetable life, and if it does not obey the law of vegetable life it sinks back into the inorganic, — that is, it dies. When the vegetable is taken into the animal, the vegetable becomes animal, — that is, it becomes subject to the law of animal life. The cow does not become grass, but the grass becomes cow, and, being cow, becomes part of the animal existence and subject to the laws of animal life; and if the laws of animal life are not obeyed, that which was life sinks back into the inorganic again, — that is, it dies. Similarly, when, in the process of development, man rises out of the animal stage and becomes a man, when he comes into the condition in which he knows the moral truth, and sees it, and is conscious of it, he comes under the law of the moral life, as the inorganic taken into the vegetable comes under the law of the vegetable, as the vegetable taken into the animal comes under the law of the animal. The human, the moment it passes the invisible boundary line and becomes human, comes under the law of the human, — that is, under the law of God, under the law of right and wrong. Moral law is dependent, therefore, upon moral development. What is right in one stage of development becomes wrong when the individual has passed into a higher stage of development. The law of the animal is superseded by the law of the spiritual. This fact we all recognize. "Gluttony is not sin in a hog; the greater glutton, the better the breed. Combativeness is not sin in a bull-dog; the bitterer fighter, the better the dog. To heap up wealth for another to enjoy after they are dead is not sin in the bees; the more they gather and the less they give, the more valuable the hive. To spend life in mere pleasure of song and sunshine is not sin in the bird; the more careless the songster, the sweeter the companionship. But to man there is a higher life possible than to feed with the hog, fight with the dog, gather with the bee, or sing with the birds; it is as he comes to a knowledge of this higher nature that he comes to a knowledge of good and evil." [1] We come to Mount Sinai when we come to the sense of right and wrong. Violation of this law

[1] *Evolution of Christianity*, p. 225.

is sin, and sin is fall, and fall is fall downward, not upward.

Did Adam fall, six thousand years ago? It is immaterial. Certainly if we found the story of a garden with one fruit by eating which a man would make himself immortal, and with another fruit which would give him a consciousness of good and evil, with a serpent which talked to him, and with a God who walked in the garden and from whom the man attempted to hide, — if we found that in Greek, or Roman, or Hindu, or Norse literature, we should say, That is beautiful fable; what truth can we find in it? And I do not see any reason why, finding it in Hebrew literature, we should not say, That is beautiful fable; what truth is in that fable?

Neither the author of Genesis, nor any one in the Bible for him, claims that his account of the creation was revealed to him. There is no reason to think that it was so revealed, unless a purely traditional theology constitutes such reason. Even if we suppose that Genesis was written by Moses, three or four hundred years elapsed between the latest incident in Genesis and the time of Moses. Moreover, Assyrian tablets have been discovered which were in existence a thousand years before the time of Moses, and which contain analogous accounts of the Creation, the Fall, and the Deluge. For these

reasons the modern Biblical scholar who believes
in what is called progressive revelation regards
the Book of Genesis as a collection of prehistoric
traditions rewritten. The value of the book
consists, not in its scientific accuracy respecting
creative processes, but in the religious spirit with
which these ancient traditions are rewritten, so
as to make them vehicles of moral and spiritual
truth. In a sense it is true, scientifically, that
God has made man out of the dust of the earth,
— that is, out of lower and earlier forms, reaching back through various transformations even
to the inorganic ; and has breathed into him the
breath of life, — that is, in him is a spirit which
links him to the Divine. But the mechanical
conception of this process, which was apparently
in the mind of the writer of Genesis, is far tran-
scended in sublimity by the conception of this
process entertained by the modern evolutionist.

Innocence, temptation, fall, sin — this is the
biography of every man, save only Him who
passed from innocence to virtue through temptation, yet without sin.   Man cannot grow from
innocence to virtue without temptation ; he cannot experience temptation without a possibility
of sin, — that is, of yielding to temptation ; and
yielding to temptation is fall. Every man
when he yields to temptation and sins falls from
a higher to a lower, from a spiritual to an ani-

mal condition. He falls back from that state
from which he had begun to emerge. It is true
that the animal man is worse in his animalism
than the animal from which he has emerged or
is emerging. The ferocity of the tiger is no
match for that of the ferocious man ; the intem-
perance of the brute is far less than that of the
brutalized man. How can it be otherwise when
the higher powers which God has conferred upon
him are subordinated to and made the instruments of his animalism ?

Sin, then, is not a means to good. It is not
"good in the making." The fall is not a "fall
upward." Every yielding to temptation is a hindrance, not a help, to moral development ; but
every temptation offers what, rightly employed,
is an indispensable means of moral development.
For all moral development is through temptation to virtue. There can be no virtue without
temptation ; for virtue is victory over temptation. An untempted soul may be innocent, but
cannot be virtuous, for virtue is the choice of
right when wrong presses itself upon us and demands our choosing. How can we have courage,
unless there is danger and apprehension of the
danger ? How can we have patience, unless
there are burdens to be borne and a desire to
remove the burdens ? How can we have fidelity, unless there is some trust to be maintained

and some temptation calling on us to leave the
trust and be false to it? The scorn of "goody-
goody" is justified, for "goody-goody" is innocence, not virtue; and the boy who never does
anything wrong because he never does anything
at all is of no use in the world. Temptation
is struggle, and virtue emerges from struggle.
And we cannot have the choice of right without
the possibility of doing wrong; and choosing
wrong is sin; and .sin is fall; because it is
choosing the animal from which we are emerging rather than the spiritual condition into
which we have partially emerged.

Does this take away the reality — the awful
reality — of sin, or remove it from our consciousness? It brings sin closer to our consciousness
and makes it more real. A familiar story may
illustrate this : The elder Dr. Tyng was very
fond of children. He was preaching one Sunday in his Sunday-school room to his children.
He was not an evolutionist; he lived before the
doctrine of evolution was known; and as he was
a very orthodox clergyman, it is not probable
that he would have been an evolutionist if it
had been known. Nevertheless he was preaching evolution without knowing it. He said to
the children: "There is the serpent, who goes
in sinuous, crooked ways — that is the liar;
there is the hog, who eats and eats, and cares

not for anything but eating — that is the glutton ; there is the little boy or girl who likes to pass before the glass and see how beautiful he or she is — that is the peacock ; and there is the passionate child who cannot control his temper and flames out on every provocation — that is the tiger." When he had finished his sermon and announced the hymn, the children started not all together ; his face flushed and he struck the book a blow, and cried out, " Stop ! stop ! stop ! " and a little girl back in the room, standing on the pew, reached forward, and, pointing her finger, called out, " Tiger ! " Dr. Tyng laid down his book, walked down the aisle, and took the little girl in his arms. He loved little children. No girl would have come to his arms under those circumstances if she had not known his love. He brought her back to the platform, and, holding her in his arms, he said, " Children, she has told the truth ; I have been fighting the tiger all my life, and I have not got control of him yet ; do not let the tiger get control over you." If a minister who is orthodox of the orthodox desires to bring home to children the fact of sin, and a little girl understands the preaching and has it brought home to her, and the preacher is preaching evolution, is it not right to say that the doctrine of evolution does not take away the consciousness of sin ?

It brings that consciousness nearer. The origin of sin does not lie in remote history. Sin is not a strange, mystic fact. Every man is two men, — a divine man and a human man, an earthly man and a super-earthly man; he is linked to the lower, out of which he is emerging ; he is linked to the upper, toward which he is tending. We carry the animal with us. When we indulge our appetite, or our greed, or our covetousness, or our pride, or our vainglory, or our selfishness, we are falling back into the animal, from which we are not yet emerged. Every man is two men, — a centaur, part animal, part man. Some have almost outgrown the animal, and some have a very small man's head on a very large beast's body.

"O wretched man that I am! who shall deliver me from this body of death?" I have read a tragic story of a Russian prisoner working in the mines chained to a fellow-prisoner who died, and for forty-eight hours he remained in that mine chained to a corpse. So Paul says of himself : I am chained to a corpse ; who shall deliver me from this dead body? One may be an evolutionist, he may believe that the individual emerged from a lower animal, he may believe the whole race has emerged from a lower animal condition, and yet he may believe that in this emergence every individual comes under divine law, and that every violation of that divine law is a sin, and every sin is a falling back into the animal condition ; and the only hope of himself and the only hope of the race is in the power that shall lift him up and out of his lower self into his higher, truer, nobler self, until he shall be no longer a son of the animal, but in very truth a son of God.

CHAPTER IV

THE EVOLUTION OF REVELATION

It is said of Jesus that He grew in wisdom and in stature. He did not know everything in the beginning. His wisdom was a growth. This is the universal law of the individual, who always grows in his knowledge of what we call religious truth, no less than in his knowledge of what we call secular truth. He is no more born with an accurate knowledge of God, truth, purity, righteousness, than with an accurate knowledge of geology, geography, astronomy, history, or language. The simplest intellectual declarations respecting God are unmeaning to a little child, — as, God is a Person. The simplest spiritual declarations respecting God mean but little — as, God is love. To the child in the infant class this does not and cannot mean what it means to the grandmother, who has passed through all the phases of love, and learned in the school of experience all the meaning of love. Does one ask, What does Christ mean by saying that we must become as little children if we

would enter the kingdom of heaven ? He means
that, however much we know, we must be eager
to learn more. Does any one ask, What does
He mean by the saying, Of such is the kingdom
of heaven ? He means, out of such eagerness
to learn more, the kingdom of heaven is developed in the soul. We all practically recognize
the truth that the child must grow into the
knowledge of God, truth, duty.

The evolutionist believes that the race has
grown, as the individual grows, into the knowledge of God and His righteousness. He does
not believe that there was a perfect revelation
at first which man lost and is gradually recover-
ing. He believes that there has been an increasing capacity to receive religious truth, and
therefore an increasing understanding of it.

We all believe that there has been such a
gradual development in all knowledge except
that which we call religious. I have, indeed,
heard of a minister who assured his congregation of his belief that Adam was acquainted
with the telephone. But this does not represent
the current belief in the ministry. That mankind has made a gradual, though by no means
steady, progress in its knowledge of the arts and
sciences, of the laws of health, of the conditions
of social progress, of political organization, of
commercial laws, no one questions. But these

involve a knowledge of ethics, — or the laws of
right and wrong, — and are involved in a knowledge of God, since all life is a manifestation of
Him. It is as impossible to separate life into its
constituent elements, as to separate a river into
its separate drops. The man grows; one part
is not instantly created and another part aban-
doned to growth. So the race grows; one part
is not instantly created and another part aban-
doned to growth. In other words, conscience,
reverence, faith, hope, love, are as subject to
the laws of growth as the intellectual faculties
or the social impulses. And only as these divine
capacities grow is a knowledge of the divine
possible. It is as impossible to put a saint's
knowledge of God into a savage by an instantaneous process, as to put into him a scientist's
knowledge of nature. The proposition is un-
thinkable. If one believes in the evolution of
man, he must believe in the evolution of inspiration and revelation.

To affirm that inspiration and revelation are
gradual processes is not to deny their reality.
To affirm that it is impossible to separate them
in human education from what we call the natural or secular elements is not to discard them.
The tree is dependent for its growth on both the
juices of the earth and the light of the sun. It
is not possible so to analyze the tree as to declare

what portions are dependent on the earth and
what on the sun. Still less is it possible even
to conceive of the sun as doing its work instantly
and creating its share of the completed tree,
and then leaving it, suspended, so to speak, in
airy nothingness, awaiting the development of
other parts by the slow process of earthy growths.
As little is it possible to separate the religious
from the secular, the revealed from the unre-
vealed, or even to imagine the divine truth instantly created in a mind not yet grown large
enough to apprehend such truth. A people who
believed that Palestine was the world, and that
the sun and moon and stars were created as
luminaries to give it light, could not possibly receive that conception of the greatness of God
which is correlated with, and in some measure
grows out of, the modern conception of an illimitable universe. The degree of inspiration which
the race can receive at any period is dependent
upon the spiritual capacity it has attained. The
degree of revelation possible to man or through
man depends upon the intellectual and spiritual
stature of the man.

What do we mean by inspiration? What by
revelation?

Inspiration is inbreathing. It is an uplifting
influence of one spirit on another spirit. A congregation listens to an inspiring address, an

audience to inspiring music. We are inspired
by reading the records of past heroism. Emotions, thoughts, feelings, pass from mind to
mind. One soul breathes life into another soul;
God breathes his life into us all. This is inspiration; the elevating or clarifying influence
which one spirit may have upon another spirit.
Belief in divine inspiration is belief that God's
spirit has such an influence on human spirits.

Revelation is unveiling. It is the disclosure
of some truth not known before. There may
be inspiration without revelation; there may be
revelation without inspiration. One may be
inspired and yet get no new view of truth; one
may get a new view of truth and not be inspired.
For the truth may not be inspiring. It may be,
indeed, the reverse, — it may be depressing. Inspiration, then, is the influence of one spirit —
and especially of the Divine Spirit — upon other
spirits. Revelation is the unveiling of truth
before not disclosed. To a considerable extent,
the Church formerly believed in revelation other
than through inspiration. The Christian evolutionist believes in revelation only through inspiration. A simple illustration will perhaps make
this clear.

When I went to college we studied chemistry
sitting in our seats, while the professor of chemistry revealed certain chemical truths to us, per-

forming the operations in the laboratory for us
while we looked on. We saw them, went away,
— and forgot what we had learned. To-day the
student of chemistry goes into the laboratory
himself. The teacher does not directly reveal
the truth to him, but patiently inspires him to
study for himself ; encourages him, guides him,
directs him, shows him how to make his own
investigations. Under the influence of that
guidance, that direction, that counsel, that inspiration, the student works out the chemical laws
for himself as though he were a new investigator.
He also gets a revelation. But it is a gradual
revelation, under the inspiring influence of a
teacher. The modern Christian evolutionist believes that revelation has been made in this manner to the world ; that God has inspired men in
their quest for truth, and that under that inspiration, studying, meditating, laboring, they find
their way to the truth.

The evolutionist, then, believes that the truths
taught in the Bible have been unveiled by God
and man working together. God has put His
children in the world, as pupils are put in a
laboratory, and has set them to work on the
great problems of life — Who am I ? What
does this world mean ? Who is over me ? What
are the laws of the moral life ? How must I
conduct myself toward my neighbor ? How must

he conduct himself toward me? What is our
future destiny? These problems God has left
us to work out for ourselves, by our own quest,
under His patient, guiding, inspiring influence.
The Bible is a record of man's laboratory work
in the spiritual realm, a history of the dawning
of the consciousness of God and of the divine
life in the soul of man. It contains the story
of his spiritual aspirations, his dim, half-seen
visions of truth, his fragments of knowledge,
his blunders, his struggles with the errors of
others, and with his own prejudices.

He who thus regards the Bible is not in the
least troubled by finding errors in it; he expects
to find such errors. They do not in the least mili-
tate against the value of the Book. It is quite
immaterial to him that the world was not made
in six days; that there never was a universal
deluge; that Abraham mistook the voice of conscience calling on him to consecrate his only son
to God, and interpreted it as a command to slay
his son as a burnt offering; that Israel misin-
terpreted righteous indignation at the cruel and
lustful rites of the Canaanitish religion for a
divine summons to destroy the worship by putting the worshipers to death; that a people
undeveloped in moral judgment could not and
did not discriminate between formal regulations
respecting camp life and eternal principles of

righteousness, such as, Thou shalt love thy neighbor as thyself, but embodied them in the same
code, and seemed to regard them as of equal
authority; that a people half emancipated from
the paganism which imagines that God must be
placated by sacrifice before He can forgive sins
gave to the sacrificial system that Israel had
borrowed from paganism the same divine authority which they gave to those revolutionary elements in the system that were destined eventually to sweep it entirely out of existence.

These and kindred errors do not have the
least tendency to shake that faith in the Bible
which regards it as containing the history of a
progressive revelation. He who so regards the
Bible does not believe that it is inerrant and
infallible, or that it claims to be so, or that
belief that the writers were inspired and the
writings contain a revelation from God to man
involves belief that it is inerrant and infallible.
To him the Bible is a collection of literature,
containing in a preëminent measure the growth
of the consciousness of God in the human soul,
as interpreted by the preëminent religious leaders of a preëminently religious people. The
descriptions of nature which it contains are
scientifically inaccurate; but they are written
by men who saw God in nature and interpreted
nature as itself an interpreter of God. Words-

worth, not Huxley, is the English analogue of
the Hebrew writer on nature. The historians
composed their histories out of such material as
they could gather, much as historians do in our
own time. These historians are often inaccurate in details; but the writers were prophets
who saw and traced the processes which God
was working out in the history of Israel. The
lawgivers enunciated some principles of eternal obligation, some provisions convenient at
the time but long since obsolete, and some laws
because, as Christ said, of the hardness of the
people's hearts, — that is, because the people
were not ready for anything better; but they
sought to interpret and apply to the life of the
nation the divine principles of righteousness in
so far as they understood these principles and
their application was practicable in their time.
The fiction of the Bible — the historical ro-
mances in the Old Testament and the parables
in the New Testament — is narrated not to en-
tertain or amuse, but to elucidate a principle or
inspire life. It is not in the literal accuracy of
science, history, law, or narrative that the value
of the Bible is to be found, but in its spirit.
And that spirit is all the more valuable to us
because it is that of men of like passions as we
ourselves are, struggling with analogous doubts
and difficulties toward God, and His truth, and

His righteousness. When the Bible is thus regarded as the sifted literature of a people whose
genius was spiritual, as the genius of Rome
was legal, as that of Greece was philosophical,
and as that of the Anglo-Saxon has been commercial, the intellectual and moral difficulties
disappear which the unscriptural dogma of infallibility has created. He who thus believes
in the evolution of revelation no longer has to
tease his mind by arguing that the creative days
were æons, that the sun standing still was an
optical delusion due to peculiar refraction of its
rays, and that some whales have throats big
enough to allow the passage of a man. He
frankly treats the stories of creation, of Joshua's
campaign, and of Jonah's adventures as literature characteristic of the childhood age of the
world, and looks for the moral lessons which
lie behind them. He no longer threatens the
integrity of his conscience by endeavoring to
reconcile the imprecatory Psalms or the massacre of the Canaanites with Christ's command to
"love your enemies." He says with Dr. John
Watson : "When the massacre of the Canaanites and certain proceedings of David are
flung into the face of Christians, it is no longer
necessary to fall back on evasion or special
pleading. It can be frankly admitted that,
from our standpoint in this year of grace, such

deeds were atrocious, and that they could never
be according to the mind of God, but that they
must be judged by the date, and considered the
defects of elementary moral processes."

The notion that inspiration and revelation
necessarily involve inerrancy and infallibility is
neither consonant with the claims of the Bible
writers nor with the general current of opinion
in the Christian Church. Christ repudiates
certain of the ancient laws, supplements others,
gives a revolutionary meaning to still others, and
affirms of others that they were concessions to
popular prejudice and sentiment. Paul declares
of himself that he knows only in part and
prophesies in part, and sees through a glass
darkly, and of Peter that he dissembled and
walked not according to the truth of the Gospel.
And Peter says of Paul that he sometimes
writes in such a way that it is hard to tell what
he means. As to the testimony of the Church,
there is no room for quotations here. Let the
reader, for both these points, read Dean Farrar's
"The Bible : its Meaning and Supremacy."

It must be frankly conceded that the question
at issue between the modern critic and the old
orthodoxy is not an insignificant one. It is not
merely a question of dates and authorship, — a
question whether Moses wrote the Pentateuch,
or how many of the Psalms were written by

David, or whether there were two Isaiahs or only
one. It is a profoundly serious one. The old
orthodoxy is right in regarding the new criti-
cism as revolutionary. It is revolutionary in its
treatment of the Bible, as the Protestant reformation was revolutionary in its treatment of the
Church. It denies the infallibility of the Bible,
as the Protestant reformation denied the infallibility of the Church. There is no infallible
authority. Infallible authority is undesirable.
God has not given it to His children. He has
given them something far better, — life. That
life can come only through struggle. There is
as little a short and easy way to truth as to virtue. The knowledge of truth can come only by
conflict with error, as the power of virtue can
come only by conflict with temptation. The
Bible is the record of the experiences of devout
men struggling toward that knowledge of God
which is life eternal; it is given to us, not to
save us from struggle, and growth by struggle,
but to inspire us to struggle that we may grow.

The Bible is not one homogeneous book,
but a collection of literature, gathered out of a
much larger range of literature, and embodying
the history of the growth of the consciousness
of God in one people, preëminent among the
peoples of their time for the perception of God.
It is the sifted utterances of the chosen prophets

of a peculiar people, peculiar in their spiritual genius. It is inspired, because the lives of the men and the hearts of the writers were lifted above the common errors and prejudices of their time ; not because they were wholly freed from human prejudice and misconception. It contains a revelation of God ; but the revelation is one in human experience, and subject to the adumbrations of human experience.

The question has been and will be asked whether he who believes in the evolution of revelation must not believe that spiritual development will not give the Church greater prophets than Israel, and greater apostles than Paul ; whether, in short, it is not time to construct a new Bible out of modern literature, which will take the place of the older Bible, composed wholly of Hebrew literature. It might, perhaps, be a sufficient reply, for one in a polemical mood, that there is no objection to the construction of such a Bible, which, when constructed, would have to take its place with the Hebrew Bible in a struggle for existence with a resultant survival of the fittest. Certainly no one who believes in the Bible as a supreme book would fear the challenge. It might be further added that most devout souls do supplement the Bible by other and more modern devotional literature. We nourish our spiritual life, not only on the

lyrics of the Hebrew Psalter, but also on those
of Faber and Whittier; not only on the stories
of Ruth and Esther, but also on that of the
Pilgrim's Progress; not only on the Gospel of
John and the Epistles of Paul, but also on the
Imitation of Christ by Thomas à Kempis and
the Holy Living and the Holy Dying by Jeremy
Taylor. The spirit of the Bible has run far
beyond the confines of that ancient literature;
and wherever one finds in spoken or in written word that which clarifies faith, strengthens
hope, and enriches love, he is finding a Bible
message, whoever interprets it to him.

But the philosopher will also perceive that
the doctrine of evolution does not necessarily
mean that the geniuses of a later age will transcend those of the earlier ages. The spiritual
evolutionist does not believe that man is the
mere creature of his circumstances. He does
not believe that "the differences between one
nation and another, whether in intellect, commerce, art, morals, or general temperament,
ultimately depend, not upon any mysterious
properties of race, nationality, or any other
unknown and unintelligible abstractions, but
simply and solely upon the physical circumstances to which they are exposed." He does
not deny the reality of character, and the effect
of character on life. He does not think that

" if W. Shakespeare had died of cholera infan-
tum, another mother at Stratford-upon-Avon
would needs have engendered a duplicate copy
of him, — just as the same stream of water
will reappear, no matter how often you pass a
sponge over the leak, so long as the outside
level remains the same." [1]   All that the believer
in evolution and revelation affirms or is called
upon by his philosophy to affirm is that spiritual
development in the Hebrew race was analogous
in its process to the spiritual development to be
seen in other peoples.   There is one characteristic feature in all such development which calls
for greater consideration than I think has yet
been given to it.   Evolution in the race appears
rather in a broadening of capacity to receive
than in a creation of capacity to impart.   At
certain epochs great men appear who, as types,
seem never to be surpassed in subsequent generations.   But the capacity to understand and
appreciate is surpassed in subsequent generations.   Greater writers of epic than Homer,
greater writers of philosophy than Plato and
Aristotle, greater dramatists than Shakespeare,
the world has never seen.   We are still studying Homer, Plato, Shakespeare, with profit;

---

[1] See Professor W. James' reply to Grant Allen in *The Will
to Believe*, p. 235, originally printed in the *Atlantic Monthly*
for October, 1880.

they are still our teachers. But more people
understand them, and understand them better,
than in their own time. So, greater interpreters
of the divine law than Moses, greater preachers
of righteousness and mercy than Amos and
Hosea, greater singers of God and the divine
life than the authors of the Psalter — let me
say, than David, whom I count the greatest of
them all — greater interpreters of the Christ
life than Paul, never have lived, — perhaps
never will live. We do not look for evolution
to produce greater poets than Homer, Dante,
Milton, and Shakespeare, nor greater teachers
of righteousness than Moses, David, Isaiah, and
Paul. But the phenomenon which we call inspiration in the realm of religious thought is not
more mysterious than the phenomenon which
we call genius in the realm of secular thought.
Perhaps the best explanation of both is that
each is a scintillation of the mind of God in and
through the minds of men. Certainly the one
is as consistent with theistic evolution as the
other. Such men are the instruments of growth ;
if the reader pleases, the seeds of future life.

The Bible, then, is a unique literature, —
peculiar not in the process of its formation, but
in the spirit which pervades it. It is a record
of the gradual manifestation of God to man and
in human experience ; in moral laws, perceived

by and revealed through Moses, the great law-
giver, and by successors imbued with his spirit
and speaking in his name; in the application
of moral laws to social conditions by great
preachers of righteousness; in human experiences of goodness and godliness, interpreted by
great poets and dramatists; and finally consummated in the life of Him who was God manifest
in the flesh, in whom the word, before spoken
by divers portions and in divers manners, was
shown in a spotless character and a perfect life.
For beyond this revelation, in His Anointed
One, of a God of perfect love abiding in perfect
truth and purity, there is nothing conceivable
to be revealed concerning Him. Love is the
highest life; self-sacrifice is the supremest test
of love; to lay down one's life in unappreciated,
unrequited service for the unloving, is the highest conceivable form of self-sacrifice. It is not
possible, therefore, for the heart of man to conceive that the future can have in store a higher
revelation of God's character, or a higher ideal
of human character, than that which is afforded
in the life and passion of Jesus Christ.

CHAPTER V

IN this chapter it is no part of my ambition, nor even of my desire, to explain the mystery of the character of Jesus Christ. Every man is in some sense a mystery to other men, and the greater the man, the greater the mystery. Who comprehends Daniel Webster? or William Shakespeare? or Plato? We do not understand genius. How much less may we be expected to understand Him who, on any estimate of His being, must be accounted the greatest moral and spiritual genius the world has ever seen? I do not, therefore, propose to offer a psychology of Jesus Christ, to measure Him, to belittle Him with definitions. I only endeavor to point out the place which He occupies in life according to the theory of a Christian evolutionist; what His relation is to what went before, and to what comes after, in the growth of the universe.

"In the beginning," says John, "was the Word, and the Word was with God, and

the Word was God." What does that mean?
What is a word? It is a manifestation of the
soul. A friend is sitting at your side in absent-
minded meditation ; you cannot imagine what
is passing through his mind. Presently he
wakes out of that absent-mindedness ; he turns
to you, looks you in the face, speaks to you,
and in that speech reveals to you what is going
on within, which has been hidden. The word
is the manifestation of the invisible spirit.
Now, the declaration of John is that God was
always a Word. He never was in absent-minded
meditation. From eternity He has been speaking ; He has always been manifesting Himself.
He did not six thousand years ago resolve to
manifest Himself in nature and so begin a creation. He has always been manifesting Himself in creation, and all the works of nature are
the revelation and the disclosure of the infinite
and eternal energy which is behind them, working out an intellectual process in and through
them. As the picture is the interpretation of
the artist, as the book is the interpretation of
the author, as the speech is the interpretation
of the orator, so the universe is the interpretation of the universal Spirit, who is speaking
through every singing bird, every blossoming
flower, every earthquake, every storm and tempest, everything beautiful, everything awful,

everything terrible, everything sublime. He
speaks in His world.

And He speaks through men ; through men
who have heard in His voice what other men did
not hear, and have felt in His presence what
other men did not feel. He spoke in past ages
to prophetic men, not only in the Hebrew nation,
but in many nations, inspiring men to a diviner
life, leading them on and up to larger living.
But preëminently He spoke to the Hebrew
nation, because that Hebrew nation was pre-
eminently ready to receive Him. Why some
soils are fertile and others are not, who can
tell ? Why some minds are fertile and others
are not, who can tell ? Why some nations are
fertile and others are not, who can tell ? This
is a part of the mystery of life. But in this
nation there arose prophets, and to these prophets this ever-speaking God spoke, and to them
He manifested Himself, and the Bible is the
gathered utterances of the inspired thinkers of
an inspired race. The Bible is not what it is
sometimes called, — the Word of God. It is
never so called in the Bible. The Word of God
includes all the languages in which God has
ever spoken — to all races, in all ages, under
all circumstances. The Bible is one of His
many words, spoken through prophets. Jesus
Christ is " the Word become flesh," — that is,

it is the manifestation of God in a human life
and character. He who has from eternity been
a self-revealing God spake in the world's history first in works, then through the prophetic
utterances of men who could better hear and
understand than could the great majority of
mankind, and at last, when the fullness of time
came, He spoke by coming into one human life
and filling it full of Himself.

Imagine for one moment that God desires to
reveal Himself to the human race; how can He
make that revelation except in the terms of a
human experience? This is what He has done.
He who, in olden time, spoke through prophets;
He who, from the beginning, was the Word,
when the race, in the spiritual process of its development, was ready for that later disclosure,
entered into one human life and filled it full of
Himself, that by looking at that life we might
comprehend what the life of God is in the world.
This is what the author of the Epistle to the
Hebrews declares: " God, having of old time
spoken unto the fathers in the prophets by divers
portions and in divers manners, hath at the end
of these days spoken unto us in His Son, whom
He appointed heir of all things, through whom
also He made the worlds." First in fragments,
in partial utterances, in broken speech He revealed little parts of Himself; these men can

comprehend only in single letters which men
must learn, — for they must understand the alphabet before they can understand the grammar
of divinity; later He comes and fills one man with
Himself and makes that One stand out in human
life as the revelation and disclosure of Himself.
This is what John says: "That which we have
seen with our eyes, that which we beheld, and
which our hands handled, concerning the Word
of life, . . . declare we unto you." As the
artist transcends all his pictures, as the orator
transcends all his speeches, so God transcends
all manifestations of God. It is that concerning the Word which the beloved disciple has
seen, and that only, which he can declare to
others. This is the meaning of the heavenly
voice: "This is my beloved Son." He is the
Son of God, because all his life is brooded by,
begotten of, proceeds from the Father. Some
of our life does, and some does not. We walk
in the world like Siamese twins, joined together,
now speaking the life of God, and now speaking the life of the world. We are Seventh of
Romans, flesh and spirit in combat with each
other; sons of the earth and sons of God
strangely commingled. He was the only begotten Son of God, because *all* his life flowed from
the divine fountain and the divine source. This
is the meaning of such declarations as that of

Paul: "In him dwelleth all the fullness of the
Godhead bodily." He was One into whom the
holy affluence of the divine nature was poured,
that He might set it forth to men. This is the
meaning of Paul's other declaration: "God was
in Christ." Jesus Christ was the tabernacle in
whom the self-revealing God dwelt, and through
whom He revealed Himself. In short, Jesus
Christ was God manifest in the flesh; that is,
such a manifestation of God as was possible in
a human life, a manifestation of what Dr. van
Dyke has well called " the human life of God."

   Jesus Christ did not manifest all the qualities
of God. There is greater manifestation of
power in the earthquake and the tornado than
was manifested in the stilling of the tempest;
greater mechanical skill manifested in the flower
than in anything that Christ wrought; greater
affluence of beneficence in every annual har-
vest than in the feeding of five thousand. But
the love, the patience, the fidelity, the truth,
the long-suffering, the heart of the Infinite and
Eternal Energy, comes to its fruition and its
manifestation in this one incomparable life, —
God manifesting Himself in a human life and
in human relations. Jesus Christ is the image
of God, — God brought within the horizon of
humanity, God adumbrated, says Mr. Beecher,
that we may look at Him; taking little steps by

our side, says Dr. Parkhurst, that we may walk
with Him. God is always manifesting Himself,
and He is manifesting Himself by successive
manifestations: first in nature; then in the
prophets; then in an inspired race; last of all,
in one man whom He fills full of Himself.

Does this divinity in Christ differ in kind, or
only in degree, from the divinity in men? There
are differences in degree so great that they become equivalent to a difference in kind; but,
with this qualification, I answer unreservedly, the
difference is in degree and not in kind. There
are not two kinds of divinity, and cannot be.
The divinity in man is not different in kind from
the divinity in Christ, because it is not different
in kind from the divinity in God. If it is, then
there are two kinds of divinity; and two kinds
of divinity means two kinds of divinities; that
is polytheism. Patience is divine, hope is divine,
purity is divine, righteousness is divine, love is
divine. There are not two kinds of patience,
hope, purity, righteousness, love, — one of which
is divine, the other human. What is the meaning of Paul's teaching but this: that we are to
have the patience of Christ; that we are to have
the righteousness of God; that we are to be pure
even as He is pure; that the divine qualities in
us are to be transcripts, reflections, repetitions,
of the divine qualities in the Everlasting Father.

This is what Paul means when he says that our righteousness is *of* God; that is, it is God's own righteousness reproduced in us; any other is a false righteousness, is indeed no righteousness at all.[1] Our divinity is the same in kind as Christ's divinity, because it is the same in kind as God's divinity; because there are not, and cannot be, two kinds of divinity. If we believe this, if we believe that evolution is simply God's method of manifesting Himself, then we need not be afraid to say that Jesus Christ is the supreme product of evolution in human history, for this simply means that Jesus Christ is the supreme manifestation which history affords of the divine.

Does, then, evolution end in the manger or at the cross? No. For Jesus Christ did not come into the world merely to be a spectacle, merely to show us who and what God is, and then depart and leave us where we were before. " I am the door," He says. A door is to push open and go through. He is the door; through Him God enters into humanity. He is the door; through Him humanity enters into God. He has come into the world in order that we, coming to some

---

[1] The righteousness, the patience, the hope, the peace, the joy, the holiness of God, or of Christ, are each declared to belong to the child of God. Romans iii. 22; 2 Thessalonians iii. 5; Romans xv. 13; Philippians iv. 7; Colossians iii. 15; 2 Thessalonians iii. 16; John xv. 11; xvii. 13; 1 Peter i. 16; Leviticus xi. 44.

knowledge and apprehension of the divine nature, coming to understand what divine justice,
divine truth, divine life, divine purity, divine
love are, may the better enter into that life and
be ourselves filled with all the fullness of God.
There is not, I think, one epithet applied to
Jesus Christ in the New Testament which, in
a modified form, is not also applied to the disciples of Christ. He is the light of the world;
and we are to be lights in the world. He is the
image of God; and we are made in God's image,
and have despoiled ourselves of that image. He
is the brightness of God's glory; and we are
ourselves to show forth the glory of God. He
is King of kings; and we are kings. He is the
great High Priest; and we are priests. He is
the only begotten Son of God; and we are sons
of God. He is filled with all the fullness of the
Godhead bodily; and we are inspired to pray
that we, too, may be filled with all the fullness
of God. And the consummation of evolution,
the consummation of redemption, — the one term
is scientific, the other theological, but the process
is the same, — the consummation of this long
process of divine manifestation, which began in
the day when the morning stars sang together,
will not be until the whole human race becomes what Christ was, until the incarnation so
spreads out from the one man of Nazareth that

it fills the whole human race, and all humanity
becomes an incarnation of the divine, the infinite, and all-loving Spirit.   What Jesus was,
humanity is becoming.

I can no longer, then, think of the incarnation
as a divine intervention in an otherwise undivine
life, beginning eighteen centuries ago, lasting
thirty-three years, and then ceasing, any more
than I can think of creation as the production
of matter, force, and law six thousand years
ago, which have since been left to work out their
own results with occasional interruptions by the
Almighty Creator.   All life is God; all force
is God.   If we could conceive that God should
cease to live, the universe would be a corpse.
No bird would sing, no fish would swim, no apple
would fall nor wind blow, no planet would move
in its appointed orbit, no man or woman would
speak or think or breathe.   The universe would
be dead, for God is its life; the world would
become one vast cemetery, for God is our life.
Evolution is not the operation of forces which
God once let loose and still controls.   The evolutionist does not believe that God created protoplasm and left protoplasm to create everything
else.   Evolution is God's way of doing things.
All force is the product of God's will and always
subject to it; what we call law is but God's
habit.   It is literally true that in Him we live

and move and have our being; so literally true
that if we ceased to be in Him we could neither
live, nor move, nor have any being. All goodness, truth, purity, valor, honor, righteousness,
all patriotism, all martyrdoms, all patient bur-
den-bearing, all conjugal love, all parental love,
all child-love, all friendships and fellowships, all
that is noble, true, and good, have their inspiration in Him, and are manifestations of Him. All
growth in goodness, as all growth in the material
universe, has its secret in His imparted life. And
Jesus Christ is the supreme manifestation of
God in past history, and the source and inspiration of all that is best in subsequent manifestations of God in Christian history.

To sum all up in a few words : God is revealing Himself to humanity. He is a Word, always speaking. He speaks through His works ;
all nature interprets Him to us. He speaks
through His prophets ; all men who have felt
the inspiration of His presence interpret Him
to us. He speaks in the one incomparable life,
lived for three short years in the little province
of Palestine that we might see how God would
live on the earth and does live in the universe,
that is, might know the heart of God. When
we stand at the grave that covers the loved form
of one dear to us, we may know that He shares
in our tears, as Jesus Christ shared in the tears

of Mary and Martha at the grave of Lazarus.
When we have sinned and are bearing the
shame of our sin in our anguish-stricken hearts,
we may know that He feels toward us as Christ
felt toward the blushing woman to whom he
said, " Go in peace, and sin no more." When
we come into our church service, and then go
from it to the street to oppress the poor, cover-
ing our iniquity by our garments of piety, and
deflect our own consciences from condemnation
by our prayers and our hymns, we may see
the divine finger of His scorn pointed at us
and hear the thunder of His tones, " Scribes
and Pharisees! hypocrites! who devour widows'
houses, and for a pretense make long prayers."
And all this is that He may make that other
and supreme revelation of Himself in our own
consciences ; that He may enter into the temple
of our own hearts ; that He may sit at our fire-
side ; that He may talk with us as a friend
talks with a friend, face to face ; that we may
know Him as one knows an intimate companion ; that He may be to us " closer than breath-
ing, nearer than hands and feet ; " that He may
come to be " not so far as even to be near ; "
that He may be one with us and we one with
Him, as Christ was one with the Father. And
this revelation of Himself which God has been
carrying on from the beginning of creation

down to the present time will not be consummated until He has reared out of these sons of clay children of God like to the Christ, not only in the walk and the outer life and circumstance, but in this, that God is in them and they in God, in one sweet, sacred, perfect fellowship.

CHAPTER VI

REDEMPTION BY EVOLUTION

WHAT is redemption? What do we mean
by this word which has come now to be a theological word, but in its original was not? Of
course it is a figure. Practically all theological
words are figures. They are metaphors. Redemption is a figure derived from captivity.
A man is captured by brigands in Italy. He is
carried off into the mountains and kept there.
Messages are sent to his friends; they must
raise a purse of money and send to the brigands; if they do not, the man will be kept a
captive there, or he will be put to death. The
friends raise money and ransom or redeem the
captive from the brigands and set him free, and
then he returns to his home and his friends
again. He has been bought with a price; he
has been redeemed. This figure has been employed by the Bible to illustrate one phase of
" God's way of doing things." God redeems
the human race. The question whether the
payment of a price, the rendering of a sacrifice,

is consistent with evolution, is a question to be
considered hereafter. In this chapter I simply
wish to lay open before the reader the evolutionary conception of redemption. The question to be considered is not, Is the doctrine of
redemption, as stated in the New Testament,
a scientific doctrine? for the Bible does not
deal with science. The Bible is a book written,
for the most part, by poets and prophets, and
the very word redemption is a poetic figure.
The question is whether, in an evolutionary
conception of life, as a growth, there is anything
that justifies this figure, any analogue in that
life, anything to which that figure may legiti-
mately and properly be applied.

In the Biblical representations there are three
kinds of brigands from which we are redeemed.
We are said to be redeemed from the flesh, or
the body, or the sinful flesh ; we are said to be
redeemed from our iniquities or transgressions ;
and we are said to be redeemed from the hand
of our enemies. Is there anything in evolution,
anything in the gradual development of man
by regular processes from lower to higher stages
of moral development, by forces resident within
the men themselves, that justifies the figure of
redemption from the body, from iniquity, from
enemies?

Evolution believes that man is emerging from

an animal condition. The body is the animal
out of which he is eventually to be developed.
The animal still clings to him. It is at once
a help and a hindrance. It is a help to his
spiritual development because it is a hindrance,
and because the spiritual development comes by
battle, and in no other way. There is no possible way by which a man can acquire temper-
ance unless he has appetites to be subdued; no
way by which he can acquire self-control, unless
he has animal passions to be controlled; no way
by which he can acquire courage, unless he has
timidity to be overcome. There must be the
temptation within as well as the moral nature
within, or the moral nature cannot be developed,
for it is developed only by conflict with the
temptation. First of all, then, man is an emerging and developing being, drawn out from,
lifted up from, a lower animal condition. He
is in battle with his own body. He is like the
butterfly emerging from the chrysalis; like the
bird pecking its way out of the shell; like
the seed breaking its husk and emerging from
the ground. The seed is in captivity to the
ground, and must be emancipated; the bird
is in captivity to the shell, and must be freed
from its imprisonment; the insect is in captivity
to the chrysalis, and must break from its prison-
house. And as the plant is not a plant until it

has broken away from the soil and come into the sunlight, as the bird is not a bird until it has broken out of the shell and come into the air, as the butterfly is not a butterfly until it has escaped from the chrysalis, so not until the man has broken away from the animal and come out of it and conquered it and subdued it is he truly a man. The evolution of the spirit is itself redemption from the flesh.

This redemption is like evolution, first, in that it can be accomplished only by a power working within. It is not by asceticism; not by starving the body; not by making it a poorer, a weaker, a feebler body; not by less body, but by a stronger spiritual nature. The power that is to redeem him must be a power working within, not without. The bird must peck its own way through the shell; the seed must break its own way through the soil; the butterfly must push its own way through the chrysalis. If you break the shell before the bird is ready to be hatched, it will be but a dead bird. So the soul must have within itself the power of its own deliverance. It is Christ *in* us who is the hope of our glory.

We are redeemed also, according to Scripture, from our transgressions and our sins. We have inherited them from the past; or we have taken them upon ourselves by our own habits;

we have surrendered ourselves to bondage. And now we are struggling to escape from this captivity. We must be redeemed from it; must be set free; and we must be set free from this sin by a power within ourselves. We continually try some easier and shorter way, and never succeed. We think if we can only take the temptation away from men, men will be virtuous. We are mistaken. Men are made virtuous by confronting temptation. The mother who tries to keep her child away from all temptation simply prepares the boy for a terrible fall when he gets old enough to leave the home. It is not by taking away the bonds, it is by giving strength to the man that he may break the bonds, that he is redeemed. Every man is like a Samson bound by his enemies, and he must acquire the strength within himself to break them. God does not break them, He gives us strength to break them. He does not set free this man, caught by brigands, and leave him in the Alps to be caught by some other brigands. He puts in his hand a musket, and says to him, " Fight your way to liberty." The power of redemption is the power of God in the soul. The evolutionary conception of religion differs from the old theology radically in this respect. The old theology — not, indeed, all old theologians, for the so-called new theology is, as Dr. A. V.

G. Allen has clearly shown, as old as the old theology; but what is currently called the old theology — regarded redemption as something done for man in heaven outside of him; the new or evolutionary theology regards redemption as something done for man within him. The one is what philosophers call objective; the other is what philosophers call subjective. Redemption is wrought *for* man by the spirit of God *in* man, making a man of him and giving him power to be master over himself. The control wrought by redemption is *self* control.

We are redeemed, in the third place, from our enemies. For we are in an enemy's country. That which binds us is not merely the animal from which we are emerging, not merely the temptations which we have taken upon ourselves by our own habits or which have been imposed upon us by our inheritance, but our companions and the life that is about us. And this redemption also must be a power working within. How shall the city and the state and the nation be redeemed from corrupt politicians? Can any foreign forces do it? Can any czar, any emperor, any army from without ? It is only by a power working from within. If our great cities cannot redeem themselves from corrupt politicians, then their fate is sealed. For, in the very nature of the case, it is manhood that

is wanted, and manhood is not accomplished by
striking the chains from men's wrists and leaving them to be reduced to bondage again by
the same evil forces that enslaved them before.
We have not redeemed the African race when
we have signed the emancipation proclamation;
we must follow it up with educative and religious influences, with the school and the church.
It is not enough to give the negro the ballot;
he must be made a man; out of the manhood
will grow citizenship.

This is characteristic of the teaching of Christ
from first to last; the life must work from within
outward, not from without inward. It is only
as God works in us to will and to do of His good
pleasure that we are saved; only as the individual or society takes into itself the vital forces
that either is endued with a new life. No trans-
action wrought in heaven will redeem either
the race or the individual. Whatever is planned
in heaven must be wrought out in the soul of
man. The sun can never bring a bud to blossom or a seed to growth, except as the rays of
the sun come to the earth and put the life into
the seed and into the bud. This is one truth,
then, involved in the doctrine of redemption by
evolution: that the redemptive force is a force
within. It is God in humanity; God in the
individual soul; God intoning the conscience,

clarifying the faith, strengthening the will, making the man; and only as the man receives God into himself can he be redeemed.

The second element in the doctrine of evolution is that it is a development from a lower to a higher stage. Evolution never goes backward. The doctrine of evolution recognizes conditions in which there is no growth; but that is called arrested development. It recognizes conditions in which there is a falling back into the conditions out of which emergence has taken place; but that is called degeneracy. Both arrested development and degeneracy are recognized by the evolutionist, but they are not parts of, they are hindrances to evolution. Evolution is not restoration.

John Milton, having told the story of the fall in "Paradise Lost," wrote "Paradise Regained," and thus he interpreted the doctrine of redemption : —

> " I, who erewhile the happy garden sang
> By one man's disobedience lost, now sing
> Recovered paradise to all mankind,
> .   .   .   .
> And Eden raised in the waste wilderness."

To some extent, at least, the old theology so conceived redemption. Man sinned and fell in Eden. Redemption is to recover him and put him back into the condition from which he fell.

Evolution cannot be reconciled with that theory ;
with the hypothesis that man was perfect, that
he fell, and that he is to be put back into the
perfect condition from which he fell.   That is
not evolutionary.   Nor can I reconcile it with
the Bible.   I cannot find from cover to cover in
the Bible the suggestion that man is to be put
back again, that he is to be restored to Eden.

The   Bible   always   anticipates   something
higher, larger, nobler than was ever known in
the past.   When Abraham goes out of the land
of paganism to a land he knows not what, he
is not called back to Eden.   When Moses calls
the children of Israel out of the land of Goshen
into the Promised Land, it is to a new land
that is to be opened up to them ; their looking
back is continually reprobated and condemned.
When the exiles are called out of Babylon, it is
not with any conception that the old condition
of things is to be restored ; it is to a new and
larger glory, when " Gentiles shall come to thy
light, and the nations to thy rising."   When
Christ comes, He never bids His disciples look
back for the golden age.   He tells them of a
kingdom to come, not of a kingdom that has
been.   He tells them that greater works than
He has done, His disciples shall do ; the future
has more for them than the past.   Paul never
suggests that the race is to go back to Eden, to

Isaiah, to David, to Moses. His call is always toward a nobler future. Finally, the last book of the Bible is a prophetic book; the garden it portrays is not the garden of Eden. In this garden of the Apocalypse the very leaves are for the healing of the nations, and the fruit is of many kinds, yielded every month, and all freely to be plucked; and alongside this garden is the great city, the New Jerusalem, the fruit of centuries of Christian civilization.[1]

The redemption, then, by evolution corresponds with the redemption described in the Bible. Neither proposes to restore the past; both propose to push forward to the future. We cannot go back politically. It is idle for Carlyle and Ruskin to lament the days of feudalism and call on us to go back to hero-worship. Out of the past a better present has been evolved, and out of the present a nobler future is to be evolved. We cannot go back politically to Jefferson's democracy, or Hamilton's conservatism. If Hamilton were here to-day, he would not be the Hamilton he once was. If Jefferson were here to-day, he would not be the Jefferson he once was. The future has more for this country than the past ever had, and the nation must press forward to the future, not turn lamentingly back to the past.

[1] See *Evolution of Christianity*, chap. i. pp. 13–20.

We cannot go back intellectually. We are
not to go back to the creeds of the past; not to
the sixteenth century, not to the fourth century.
God has been keeping his children at school for
eighteen centuries. They ought to know more
after eighteen centuries of education than they
did in the first century. And they do. We are
more competent to create a system of theology
to-day than they were who made the Westmin-
ster Confession of Faith; more competent than
they were who made the Nicene Creed. Many
are they who lament the childlike faith of the
past. We never can have the childlike faith of
the past, and we are not to wish for it. We are
to wish for the manhood faith of the future; not
the unshaken faith of the babe, — the shaken
faith of the man; not the little oakling which is
putting its leaves above the ground, — the great
strong oak that has breasted the storms and run
its roots down deep, because the storm has beat
upon it. We ought to be more devout because
of Robert Ingersoll. Not because he is an edu-
cator in devotion, but because the shaken faith
should be stronger than the unshaken, and we
should have our roots so laying hold of God
Almighty that blasts of tempestuous doubt
shall only make them take a stronger hold.

As organically and socially and intellectually,
so spiritually we are to move forward. Progress

is not toward innocence. Innocence once lost cannot be recovered. Spiritual progress is from innocence through temptation to virtue. The struggle is essential to the victory, and the victory lies in the future. Out of the condition of innocence, when we had not sinned because we had not been tempted, we are carried by successive stages forward, if we are true to ourselves, to our education, and to our opportunity, to the manhood which masters temptation and is by it made strong.

What is true of the state, the Church, the individual, is true of the race. Men ask concerning the world, " Is it worse, or better?" It is both. The drunkenness of to-day, since the invention of distilled liquors, is worse than the drunkenness in ancient Rome. They did not know delirium tremens, and we do. When men learned to write, they acquired a new method of fraud, — forgery. With banks and credit systems came in the possibility of defalcation; with science, explosives and dynamite. The public school makes some men better, some men worse. Power used for virtue is good, used for vice is evil, — and development is power. The temptations of life are far greater in this nineteenth century than they were in the sixteenth or the first. The temptations the adult man has to meet with in society, in business, in the family, are far greater than the temptations which assailed him when a little child four or five years old, protected by his mother. The passage of life is from innocence, through temptation, to virtue, and every new virtue acquired is only preliminary to a new battle to be begun.

This is redemption, — the development of the whole man. In it we come, through all the conflict of life, unto a perfect manhood in Christ Jesus, into clearness of vision, largeness of knowledge, strength of will. Redemption makes the very enemies of spiritual life instruments of spiritual life. Redeemed, we become conquerors; nor is that all: "more than conquerors." More than a conqueror? How is that possible? Napoleon, landing on the shores of France from Elba, met successive detachments of Bourbon troops sent out to capture him, and detachment after detachment, as it came to him, swept round to his rear and swelled his ranks to give him victory. He was more than conqueror. This is what redemption, or evolution, — one term is theological, the other is scientific, — does for man. In redemption, in spiritual evolution, the machine and the corrupt politicians become the instruments of our victory; the purer state is achieved by the battle with corrupt forces. The temptations that assail us become forces for the development of our manhood ; the chisel that strikes against us perfects the image of the Christ in us. The cohorts of evil are converted into the recruits of virtue, and by temptation we conquer a virtue that is immeasurably sublimer than innocence.

CHAPTER VII

WHY, in a world made and ruled by a beneficent being, should there be suffering, — not acci-
dental, incidental, occasional, but wrought into
the very woof of life? The first sound of the
babe is a cry; the last sound of the dying man
is, ordinarily, a sigh or groan; and from the
cradle to the grave the sad refrain of sorrow
sounds. Neither the merry music of pleasure,
the clatter of industry, nor the noise of battle
can effectually drown it. We can understand
some aspects of this mystery. Why sin should
bring with it penalty we can understand; why
imperfection should require suffering as a discipline for its removal we can understand. But
the innocent suffer more than the guilty: the
mother more than the wayward son; the hero on
the battlefield laying down his life for the nation, or suffering racking pain in the hospital,
more than the ambitious politician who provoked
the war; the martyr offering his life for the
Church more than the bigot who fires the fagots.

How is this? Why should innocence suffer as well as guilt — often more?

We might more easily understand this if suffering belonged only to the lower forms of life, and we gradually emerged from it. But, on the contrary, the lowest forms of life suffer the least; the higher we rise in life the keener is the anguish, the bitterer the pain. This is the problem we are to consider. I do not attempt to solve this problem. I only attempt to show that not only suffering, but vicarious suffering, the suffering of the innocent for the guilty, is an essential element in the process of growth. It is not peculiar to religion, it is a part of the mystery of life. I do not seek to explain the problem of suffering, I seek simply to correlate it with the universal mystery.

Darwinism is not evolution, though it is often in popular imagination confounded with evolution. Darwinism stands for the doctrine that the progress of life has been due to a struggle for existence in which the fittest have survived and the unfittest have perished. I do not affirm that this is a complete epitome of Darwin's teaching. It is immaterial for the purpose of this chapter whether it is so or not. It is for this doctrine of struggle for existence and survival of the fittest that the word Darwinism stands in popular language; and evolution stands for very much more.

" Darwinism," says the " Century Dictionary,"
" is in general the theory that all forms of
living organisms, including man, have been derived or evolved by descent, with modification
or variation, from a few primitive forms of life
or from one, during the struggle for existence
of individual organisms, which results, through
natural selection, in the survival of those least
exposed, by reason of their organization or situ-
ation, to destruction. It is not to be confounded
with the general views of the development or
evolution of the visible order of nature which
have been entertained by philosophers from the
earliest times."

I am not trying in this volume to show that
Christianity can be harmonized with Darwinism.
If Darwinism be accepted by any as a complete solution of the process of life, it is not so
accepted by the great evolutionists. It is only
one contribution to the philosophical conception
of the processes of life. The doctrine that struggle for existence and the survival of the fittest
is an epitome of life, that all animate nature is
wrestling, every fellow with his fellow, and that
every life depends on the destruction of some
other life, slain in the struggle by the selfishness
of the victor, is a hard and cruel view of life, and
it is not the view of the great evolutionists. Mr.
Huxley, in his notable address on " Evolution

and Ethics," distinctly disavows and repudiates
it. He maintains that when life has passed
beyond a certain imaginary line, when we have
reached that state of existence in which the
moral law begins to operate, then this struggle
for existence and survival of the fittest will no
longer develop the higher life, and a new force
must and does enter. He says : —

" As I have already urged, the practice of
that which is ethically best — what we call goodness or virtue — involves a course of conduct
which in all respects is opposed to that which
leads to success in the cosmic struggle for existence. In place of ruthless self-assertion it demands self-restraint; in place of thrusting aside,
or treading down, all competitors, it requires
that the individual shall not merely respect but
shall help his fellows; its influence is directed
not so much to the survival of the fittest as to
the fitting of as many as possible to survive. It
repudiates the gladiatorial theory of existence.
It demands that each man who enters into the
enjoyment of the advantages of a polity shall
be mindful of his debt to those who have labo-
riously constructed it, and shall take heed that
no act of his weakens the fabric in which he has
been permitted to live. Laws and moral pre-
cepts are directed to the end of curbing the
cosmic process and reminding the individual of

his duty to the community, to the protection and influence of which he owes, if not existence itself, at least the life of something better than the brutal savage." [1]

That is the utterance of one of the most famous evolutionists. Evolution is not the theory that struggle for existence and the survival of the fittest is the whole history of life. There is another and at least equally important element. The great contribution which Mr. Drummond has made to the theory of evolution is in carrying this thought of Mr. Huxley further back in history. In the " Ascent of Man " he has shown that there is another struggle than the struggle for existence, which dates from the very beginning of creation ; that there are two struggles going on contemporaneously, — the struggle for others, as he rightly calls it, and the struggle for self ; and that development of life is due to the combined struggle, — the selfish and the unselfish, the struggle for self and the struggle for others than self. It is true that he was not the first to do this. Herbert Spencer had shown that altruism runs far back in human history. But Mr. Drummond has shown this with greater clearness of statement, beauty of illustration, warmth of feeling, and more intellectual emphasis than any predecessor. " Creation," says Mr. Drum-

<hr>

[1] *Evolution and Ethics ; Collected Essays*, vol. ix. p. 81.

mond, "is a drama, and no drama was ever put upon the stage with only one actor. The struggle for life is the 'Villain' of the piece no more; and, like the 'Villain' in the play, its chief function is to react upon other players for higher ends. There is, in point of fact, a *second* factor which we might venture to call the Struggle for the Life of Others, which plays an equally prominent part. Even in the early stages of development its contribution is as real, while in the world's later progress — under the name of Altruism — it assumes a sovereignty before which the earlier struggle sinks into insignificance." [1]

Evolution, then, involves these two fundamental ideas: Struggle for Self, and Struggle for Others; Struggle for Self in all the long line of development, from the first beginnings of endeavor to maintain a mere physical existence up to the last supreme struggle with the powers of evil, out of the very struggle with which there is developed a higher moral nature; [2] and interwoven with it Struggle for Others, not introduced, as Mr. Huxley would have us think, when man reaches an ethical stage, but beginning with the very beginnings

[1] *The Ascent of Man*, p. 13. Compare also *Social Evolution*, by Benjamin Kidd, and *Moral Evolution*, by Professor George Harris.

[2] See chapter iii., "The Genesis of Sin."

of life. The first beginning of organism is
a cell, and that cell cannot reproduce itself in
the first step toward growth except by parting
with a part of itself. The cell itself becomes
divided; it gives part of its life in order that
by the very giving of this life there may be the
beginning of a growth. Evolution has its birth
in sacrifice. From that starting-point, when
the first protoplasm divides, and out of that
division there begins another and a larger life,
all the way up to the highest, life goes on by the
process of giving for others what belongs to self.
The bird does not begin in the egg, it begins in
the mother; and when the bird is in the egg,
the mother surrenders her freedom and im-
prisons herself that she may brood the egg and
develop its life; and the father bird becomes
a forager, gathering food, not primarily for
himself, but for the mother bird and for the
little unfledged birds that are to be or that have
come. The struggle of the bird in the forest
is the struggle for the birdling, — the struggle
of father and mother for others. As life rises
in the scale of being, this Struggle for Others
becomes at once more difficult and more apparent. The feeblest of all the infants is the infant
man. The infant bird can care for itself better
than the infant man. The period of caretaking
is longer in the case of the infant man. It is

kept up through successive years ; first the care
of the mere physical well-being, then care for
the intellectual and moral development. The
child exists, not because it has struggled for
existence, but because from the hour of birth
the father and the mother have struggled for
the child's existence, giving their life for the
child.

And as this process goes on, and the child
comes into the intellectual and moral realm, the
intellectual and the moral growth depend also
upon a life-giving by another. Self-educated we
call men. No man is self-educated ; he acquires
his education from some one else : from pro-
fessional teacher, from public school, from father
and mother, from companions. Some one who
has lived before him, some one who is living at
his side, is ministering to his life, and pouring
life into him. All our schools and all processes
of education are founded on this fundamental
postulate : that the life of the individual can
grow only as some one else is giving life to him.
This is not a mere individual fact, it is a race
fact. No race ever develops itself without a
higher element coming into the race and moving upon it. We have tried the experiment
of self-development in this country. The North
American Indians had noble blood in them,
and qualities of a noble manhood. We put

them into reservations; forbade the railroad
to bring enterprise, the telegraph to give intelligence, the post-office to bring the mails. With
the life of the nineteenth century shut out from
them, in our New York reservations, the Indians are to-day substantially as pagan as they
were a hundred and fifty years ago.

Life proceeds from life. This is apparently
a universal truth. Scientists are very cautious
about making general statements, — much more
cautious than theologians are, — and probably
no scientist will say that life never can proceed
except from life ; but all scientists will say this:
that, so far as we can discover, life never has
proceeded from the non-living. Always, in the
physical realm, in the intellectual realm, in
the spiritual realm, life is a gift. The secret
of growth, its starting-point, its very source, is
a struggle by one for another.

And this impartation of life, by struggle of
one for another, as we rise in the scale of life,
comes to involve self-denial, self-sacrifice. The
mother bird surrenders the joy of freedom
of flight for the greater joy of maternity.
The human mother who formerly enjoyed society shuts herself up in the nursery with
no society but the babe in her arms. The
teacher goes down from his high estate of knowledge to link himself with the ignorant pupils

before him; unless he can do this, he cannot
teach. In this respect our colleges often make
great mistakes; they look out for great scholars;
but a great scholar is often not a great teacher.
To be a great teacher one must not only have
great thoughts, but great sympathy with men
who have not great thoughts; he must know
how to come down out of himself to the pupils
before him, come into touch with them, and
pour out of his abundance into their vacuity.
That costs something, and in the moral and
spiritual realm it costs a great deal. It is
easy to give food; more difficult to give intellectual culture; most difficult of all to give
moral and spiritual life. A pure woman con-
secrates herself to the task of giving purity
to women who have lost it; does it not cost her
something? Does she not hate the impurity?
Does she not shrink from contact with it?
Does it not revolt her, as a noisome atmosphere
revolts the healthful lungs? Does she not have
to conquer her revulsion by the higher inspira-
tions of her love, that she may render this
service? Is it not absolutely certain that if
she has not that horror of impurity, has not
to battle in herself, has not to conquer her own
instinctive shrinking by her larger love, — is it
not certain that she can do nothing? An un-
sympathetic heart cannot help a sorrowing or

a sinful one; and to sympathize is to suffer
with.

What has made the Church of Christ what
it is to-day? *Our* struggles? Did *we* face
the persecutions of Nero? Did *we* flee from
the persecuting hordes in the Waldensian val-
leys? Did *we* fight the battles with the Duke
of Alva on the plains of Netherlands? Did *we*
struggle with hierarchical despotism at Worces-
ter and at Naseby? Did *we* face the cold
and the suffering of New England? Others
have struggled for us, and we have taken the
fruit of their struggles; and if our posterity
are to have a nation worthy of their possession,
it will be because in us there is also some hand-
to-hand wrestling, some self-denial, some struggle with the forces of corruption and evil in our
own time. This is the great general law which
Paul has expressed in the declaration, "The
whole creation groaneth and travaileth together
in pain until now." Vicarious sacrifice is not
an episode. It is the universal law of life.
Life comes only from life. This is the first
proposition. Life-giving costs the life-giver
something. That is the second proposition.
Pain is travail-pain, birth-pain; and it is a part
of the divine order — that is, of the order of
nature — that the birth of a higher life should
always be through the pain of another.

This is the law of God, — that is, the nature
of God. For the laws of God are not edicts
promulgated ; they are the expressions of Himself ; and the law that life comes only by the
pouring out of life through suffering is an expression of the divine nature. This is the meaning of Paul's teaching in the eighth chapter of
Romans : first, that it is the universal law that
all life is by impartation of life ; and, secondly,
that this is universal because it is divine ; that
God Himself is the great Life-giver, and gives
by His own suffering His life to the children of
men.

This, too, is what is meant by that statement
so dear to some and so shocking to others, —
that we are saved by the blood of Christ. Let
us try for a moment to disabuse our minds of
traditional opinions and see what that phrase
means looked at in the light of history. Is
"the blood of Christ" the blood which flowed
from Him at the crucifixion ? His was almost
a bloodless death ; a few drops of blood only
trickled from the pierced hands and feet ; for
the blood and water that came from the side
when the spear pierced it came after death,
when the suffering was all over. Blood, the
Bible itself declares, is life ; we are saved by
the blood of Christ when we are saved by the
life of Christ, — by Christ's own life imparted

to us, by Christ's life transmitted; and by
Christ's life transmitted, as life alone can be
transmitted, through the gateway of pain and
suffering.[1] The suffering of Jesus Christ was
not a single episode, — one short hour, one short
three years : the suffering of Jesus Christ was
the revelation of the eternal fact that God is
from eternity the Life-giver, and that giving
life costs God something, as it costs us something.

Evolution, then, certainly does teach that to
give life costs something; that the secret of
growth is the impartation of life; and this is
what the Bible means by what we call vicarious
sacrifice. I must either run the hazard of start-
ling the faith and shocking the sensibilities of
some, or else the hazard of speaking vaguely,
indefinitely, unclearly, and uncandidly, which
no teacher ever has a right deliberately to do.
I was educated to believe in what is known as
the governmental theory of the atonement. I
was brought up to believe that God had pro-

---

[1] " The blood of Christ means the inmost essence of character, the self of his self. . . . The blood of Christ, said Igna-
tius of Antioch, is love or charity. What is the blood of
Christ ? asked Livingstone of his own solitary soul in the
last months of his African wanderings. It is Himself. It is
the inherent and everlasting mercy of God made apparent to
human eyes and ears." (Condensed from Dean Stanley's
Christian Institutions, chapter vi.)

nounced certain judgments against sinful humanity, that a penalty was due for our misdeeds, that Jesus Christ came to the earth and suffered the penalty in order that God might take the penalty off from us and let us go. I not only was brought up to believe it, but I did believe it in the early years of my ministry. I believe it no longer. It is not in consonance with the teaching either of Scripture or of life. In life punishment is not taken from the guilty and put upon the innocent. The father does not put the penalty upon the mother in order that he may forgive the boy. The governor does not put the penalty upon some innocent person in order that he may sign a pardon for the guilty person. There is nothing akin to this conception of penalty and pardon in life. Nor is it to be found in the teaching of Scripture. Scripture doctrine need not always be stated in Scripture phraseology, but a doctrine which for its statement *must* use words not to be found in the Scripture may safely be looked upon with suspicion. We are asked to affirm a doctrine of expiation. The word expiation does not occur in the New Testament. We are asked to affirm our belief in vicarious suffering. The word vicarious does not occur in the New Testament. We are asked to affirm that Christ was a substitute for man. The words substitute and sub-

stitution do not occur in the New Testament.
We are asked to affirm our belief in atonement.
The word atonement does not occur in the New
Testament. It is to be found in only one place
in the Old Version, and in the New Version it
has been rendered, as it should be, "reconciliation," as it is throughout the New Testament
where the same Greek word occurs.

There is no authority in Scripture for the
doctrine that God puts the penalty due to a
guilty person upon an innocent one. We are
saved by the blood of Christ, because we are
saved by the life of Christ poured into our life;
saved by the sacrifice of Christ, because there is
no way in which life can be ministered to without the seeming sacrifice of another life ; saved
by the suffering of Christ, because there is no
way in which, from the lowest to the highest,
including God Himself, one can minister to the
life of another in the moral and spiritual realm
without suffering. I cannot find anywhere in
the Old Testament the idea of sacrifice coupled
with the idea of penalty; it is always coupled with purification. The house is corrupted
by leprosy : a sacrifice is offered. Why? To
purify the home. The priest must offer a sacrifice before he goes into the Holy of Holies.
Why? To *purify* himself and make himself
fit to enter into the sacred place. The Great

Day of Atonement comes ; two goats are led
out as nearly alike as possible ; a red cord is
tied around the horns of one to represent the
sins of the people; the sins are laid upon the
head of that goat by the priest in a prayer of
confession; then that goat is led off into the
wilderness and seen no more, and the twin goat
is slain.   What is laid on the head of the scape-
goat? Punishment? No ! not the punishment,
— the sins of the people are carried away; the
people are purified by sacrifice.   Turn from the
Law to the Prophets, and to the one chapter of
the one prophet which has more to say of Christ
as the sacrifice for sin than all other chapters
of all other prophets, — the fifty-third chapter
of Isaiah. Not from beginning to end of this
chapter is there a suggestion of deliverance from
penalty by the suffering servant of the Lord ;
he brings healing, cure, deliverance from sin.
" With his stripes we are *healed*."   " The Lord
hath laid on him the *iniquity* of us all."

If we turn from the Old Testament to the
New Testament, we find the same truth there.
Nowhere in the New Testament is the sacrifice of
Christ coupled with a statement of the removal
of punishment, — but always with the trans-
mission of life or the removal of sin.   He is the
Lamb of God which taketh away the *sins* of the
world. He is called Jesus because He saves his

people from their *sins*. His is the blood of the
New Testament, which is shed for many for the
remission of *sins*. The flesh which He gives, He
gives for the *life* of the world. The blood of
Jesus Christ *cleanseth* us from all sin. Whether
we look at the Old Testament types and figures
in sacrifice or at the New Testament's direct
teachings concerning the sufferings of Christ,
the lesson is always the same, — the suffering
of Christ is for purification, not merely, not
chiefly, perhaps not at all, for the removal of
penalty.

And surely, if there be any noble instinct in
us, any divine aspiration, any pure desire, it
cannot be satisfied by the mere statement that
punishment will be taken away. How often has
it happened in human history that the man who
has sinned has said, " I wish to be punished ; I
wish to bear the penalty." It is not the removal
of the penalty, it is the removal of the sin, humanity needs ; the animalism taken out, a new
and higher nature made master and conqueror.
It is life, not ease ; righteousness, not pearly
gates and golden streets. If we be men and
women, we do not so much care to be in heaven
as to have heaven in us.

To sum all up in a few words of restatement :
life comes only as some one is willing to give
his life ; and life can be given to the sinful only

through pain and suffering. The cross of Christ
is like a window through which the soul looking
sees the eternal facts : the Lamb slain from the
foundation of the world, God bearing the sins
and sufferings of His children through all ages,
until He shall bear them away, pouring out His
life-blood through all the ages, until, pouring it
into these our poisoned veins, He shall have
cleansed them of their impurity, filled them with
a new life-current, and made us worthy to be
called children of God. As I have passed from
that earlier, and, as it seems to me, cruder and
more artificial conception, to this later, and, as
it seems to me, profounder conception, the cross
of Christ has come to mean not less but more ;
and as I stand before it and look up into the
eyes of Him who hangs upon it, I see in Him
not merely one who has borne scourging for my
sake, but one who interprets the consummate
fact of human life, — suffering for others, in
which I now see a prophecy of the awful yet
splendid divine fact of God's infinite suffering
love. For in that cross the Crucified discloses
the eternal love of the Father, and shows Him
the Life-giver to us, His children, through the
giving of His own life for us and our salvation.

CHAPTER VIII

EVOLUTION AND PROPITIATION

WE have seen that the idea of evolution involves the idea of struggle. There is first a
"struggle for existence," and, as the result of
this struggle, a survival of the fittest and a
growth toward that which is fit to survive. An
analogous struggle is seen in the higher realms
of life. Knowledge of the truth, clearness of
apprehension and tenacity of grasp upon it, are
developed by struggle with error. Revelation
is not a divine contrivance for saving men from
struggle, but a divine incitement to and encour-
agement in struggle! Virtue is developed by
struggle with temptation. Grace is not an easy
bestowment of virtue on an unstruggling creature, but such aid as is necessary to inspire the
courage of hope and give assurance of victory.
But struggle is for others as well as for self;
the struggle of love as well as of self-interest;
the struggle of parents for their offspring, of
reformers for the State, of martyrs for the
Church. And these and kindred struggles all

point to and are prophetic of the service and
the sacrifice of the Son of God. For this struggle of love is divine. It belongs not to the in-
firmity of humanity, but is an essential element
in that process of evolution which is God's way
of doing things. It is the object of this chapter
to make clear the further truth that this struggle for others necessarily includes a struggle in
one's self; that as in the redeemed there is a
struggle within between the temptation and the
aspiration, victory in which is virtue, so there is
in every redeemer a struggle between hatred for
the sin and pity for the tempted; and that this
struggle also is not an incident of human weak-
ness, but is essential in the work of redemption;
so that without this inward struggle no redemption would be possible.

If we trace the history of the moral and spiritual development of the race, we find first and
lowest that state of mind in which sin is looked
upon with allowance, indifference, unconcern.
Men laugh at sin, or even honor it. Their gods
are lawless and wicked. The gods of classic
Greece and Rome were drunken, hateful, licentious, thieving, lying gods. What was said by
Isaiah of the Israelitish nation might have been
said of them: they were full of iniquity from
the crown of the head to the sole of the foot.
The Psalmist recognizes this low conception of

divinity, when in one of the Psalms he says,
" You thought that God was altogether such an
one as you are." There are in all our great
cities men and even women who are living in
this moral state, in whom sin awakens no remorse, to whom the drunkard is only an object
of amusement, to whom licentiousness is matter
of jest if not of admiration. There have been
epochs in human history characterized by this
moral state, even late in the Christian era. The
literature of England in the reign of Charles
the Second is full of illustrations of this death
in life.

The first step out of this condition of indifference to sin is the state of wrath and indignation against it. This indignation is almost
always aroused, in the first instance, by sins
which impinge upon the individual himself.
False witness may slander my neighbor, and I
bear it with unexemplary patience; but if he
slanders me, I am wrathful. For in the beginning nothing awakens conscience but self-love.
A man may rob my neighbor, and I shall not
be greatly troubled; but let him rob me, and I
am full of indignation, because at first the moral
nature is stirred only by selfishness. Recent history has afforded a striking illustration of this
truth. The Armenians have been massacred
by the Turks, the Greeks have risen in a futile

revolt against the Turks. The Anglo-Saxon
race has looked on with some impatience, but
with unexemplary equability of temper. Had
the victims of Turkish malevolence been an
Anglo-Saxon people, England would have been
aflame with uncontrollable indignation.

But gradually we grow out of this lower state,
in which only self-interest can arouse effectual
indignation against wrong. We begin to feel
wrath at wrong-doing which does not affect our
interests. We begin to organize against the
sins that harm others than ourselves. We feel
wrath and indignation toward a man who has
done any wickedness. That is a bad state of
society in which a mob executes the death sentence on assassins; but that is a worse state of
society in which crime goes unpunished and
there is no flambent wrath in the community
against iniquity. Mob law is not to be defended,
but mob law is the expression of a conscience not
yet dead; and where there is no wrath, and
iniquity goes unchastised of justice, then society
has gone back into animalism. Thus, out of
that state of society which characterized Rome
in the first century, in which flagrant iniquity
went unpunished, emerges that state of society
which existed in the Middle Ages, in which the
consciences of men were aroused in wrath against
iniquity, and against those forms of iniquity that

did not directly injure those who were the aven-
gers. It is true that the cruelties of the Inqui-
sition rivaled the cruelties of Nero. But they
were not as immoral. The conscience that flames
out against men, not for selfish reasons, but because it believes men have blasphemed the name
of God, indicates a better moral state than that
in which vengeance is aroused only by personal
selfishness or ambition. The wrath of conscience
is as cruel a wrath as that of covetousness, but
it is not so immoral nor so degrading.

As society is educated under the teaching of
God's Gospel, it passes by a natural reaction
from hatred of sin into simple compassion and
pity. Then we pick the drunkard out of the
gutter, and coddle him and set him up on the
platform to be straightway our teacher; for we
have now no sense of wrath against inordinate
appetite. We are overwhelmed with pity for
the murderer, with no restraining sense of justice against him, and send him gifts, — broiled
chicken and costly flowers, — and parade his
name in the newspapers almost as a hero to be
worshiped. We say that we are charitable. In
fact we have forgotten that which is the basis of
all moral character, — to *abhor* that which is
evil. As the first century represented the state
of indifference to iniquity, as the Middle Ages
represented the state of wrath against iniquity,

so this nineteenth century often represents mor-
bid sentiments of pity. We are not so much
concerned with the drunkard as with his head-
ache and his misery. We are not so much
troubled by covetousness as by poverty, and are
more eager to form anti-poverty societies than
anti-covetous societies. It is the evil which sins
bring upon men that brings sorrow to our hearts
rather than sin itself. Nor shall we come into
a moral state which is worthy of the children of
God until we have taken these two factors,
wrath against sin and pity because of sin, and
found a way to unite them in one common experience. Not merely wrath against sin and pity
for the sinner. No woman who is pure but
must have felt a sense of revulsion from the impure woman. No man who is perfectly truthful
but must have felt a sense of loathing for a liar.
No man who is honest but must have felt a
sense of antagonism, hate, wrath, indignation —
call it what you will, there are no words adequate
to express it — for the dishonest man. And yet
with this sense of indignation against that
which is iniquitous and shameful, there is also
in the heart a great pity for the sinful man.
We both hate him and sorrow for him; and out
of these two combined experiences there grows
mercy.

For mercy is not merely pity for a sinful man.

It is the pity of wrath. All our experiences of
the soul are wrought out of the antagonisms of
conflicting experience. What is patience? It is
the experience of the sensitive man whose sen-
sitiveness is mastered by a dominating love, and
therefore endures; who is roiled and tried, and
still maintains an equable temper. No man
can be patient who has not strong passions, for
patience is passion tamed. He who says, "I
know no fear," is no hero. No man knows
courage unless he does know fear, and has that
in him which is superior to fear, and conquers
it; so that out of the higher and nobler passion
— patriotism, love of children, love of truth or
right — there issues a power that subdues fear,
and makes the man conqueror. For courage is
caution overcome. So no man knows mercy
who does not know how to hate sin. For mercy
is hate pitying. It is the wrath of a great
righteousness flowing out in a great compassion.
It is the reconciliation of these two experiences,
— the experience that hates and the experience
that pities; and because it hates will destroy
iniquity, and because it pities will destroy
iniquity.

If we ever are to save our fellow men, we
must save them by this mercifulness which is a
joint experience of a great hatred because of
wrong, and a great pity also because of wrong.

Both of these elements must be within us, or we can make no step toward saving the wrong-doer. In Wagner's drama, Parsifal is besought by the wicked Kundry to accept her love and love her in return. " No," he says, " I cannot and I will not." "Come down," she says, "for one hour to my love, and take it and give your love in return," and he answers, " Were I to do it, it would be damnation both for you and for me." There is no way he can save her except he retain the hatred for the iniquity in her; for if he sacrifices that, he will not save her, he will only destroy himself. If he did not pity her, his wrath would destroy her; if he did not revolt from her, his unwrathful pity would doom both her and him to a common destruction. For it is never possible for any one to save another unless he has in him both of these elements.

When slavery ruled this nation in North and in South, in the shop, in the Church, in the council chamber, then a few men rose up in their wrath and in their pity. They could have done nothing if they had not felt a great wrath against slavery ; if they had not felt it as though it were their own sin ; if the weight of the whip had not been as on their own backs, and the marks of the chain as on their own wrists, and the ignominy of the auction-block had not been as their own. They said, This is our shame,

because we are Americans and this is the sin of
America. Without this wrath against slavery,
they never could have become leaders in the
redemption of the Nation. There are pure and
noble men and women working among the more
wretched populations of our great cities, to redeem them from squalor, ignorance, vice, and
crime. They have worked five years, ten years,
twenty years. Does the filth seem less filthy?
the shame less shameful? the wickedness less
wicked? the grog shop, the gambling hell, the
house of ill-fame, the crowded, filthy tenement
house — do they seem less hateful? If the soul
has grown hardened to these things; if, by reason of familiarity, contempt and indifference
have grown up; if the filth and profanity and
drunkenness and licentiousness no longer stir
indignation, the missionary is no longer fit for
missionary work. He must have this double
spirit; he must have both the flames that con-
sume and the tears that quench.

It is only by human experiences that we can
interpret the Divine. We are certainly not to
think of God as one who is wrathful and who
has to be appeased by some one outside of Himself. We are certainly not to think of Him as
though He were an infinite and eternal Shylock
who must have his pound of flesh, and is appeased only because there is at his side a more

merciful Bassanio who will give the price and
let Antonio go free. But neither are we to
think of Him as though good - nature were
synonymous with love, as though He were an
indifferent and easy-going God, who cares more
for the present happiness than the real character of His children ; who says, "You have
done some wrong things, you have committed
some faults, you have fallen into some errors,
you have some stains upon you ; but we will let
it all pass ; it is of no great consequence." We
shall never enter into the mystery of redemption
unless we enter in some measure into these two
experiences of wrath and pity, and into the
mystery of their reconciliation. We must real-
ize that God has an infinite and eternal loathing of sin. If the impure and the unjust, the
drunkard and the licentious, are loathsome to
us, what must be the infinite loathing of an
infinitely pure Spirit for those who are worldly
and selfish, licentious and cruel, ambitious and
animal ! But with this great loathing is a great
pity. And the pity conquers the loathing, appeases it, satisfies it, is reconciled with it, only
as it redeems the sinner from his loathsomeness,
lifts him up from his degradation, brings him
to truth and purity, to love and righteousness ;
for only thus is he or can he be brought to God.
The Old Theology has, it seems to me, griev-

ously erred in personifying these two experiences; in imputing all the hate and wrath to the Father and all the pity and compassion to the Son. But the New Theology will still more grievously err if it leaves either the wrath or the pity out of its estimate of the divine nature, or fails to see and teach that reconciliation is the reconciliation of a great pity with a great wrath, the issue of which is a great mercy and a great redemption.

Once upon a time, so runs the Roman legend, there came a gulf in the city of Rome. The oracles were consulted and said that the gods were angry, and that, to appease them, Rome must cast her most precious thing into this great gulf, or Rome would be swallowed up. Women brought their jewels, and men their gold, and priests their sacred utensils from the altar; and still the gulf grew wider. At last one young man said to himself, "What is the most precious thing in Rome? — what but its youth?" So he armed himself as for battle, and mounting on a charger, while the people gathered round in awe, he rode straight into the chasm; and then it closed over him and Rome was safe. That story has often been used as an illustration of the love of Christ redeeming us from the wrath of God. But that is paganism. If that is our notion, we have two gods; we are poly-

theists. If that is our notion, we shall dread
the Father and desire to escape Him, for He is
an angry God from whom we must be saved.
If this is our notion, we shall not be inspired
by Christ to love the Father, but shall transfer
our love from the Father to the Christ, from
the angry God who is to be appeased to the
Curtius who has leaped into the chasm to appease Him.

In the classical Greek the gods are said to be
appeased or satisfied or propitiated ; but in the
New Testament God is never said to be propitiated, nor is it ever said that Jesus Christ
propitiates God or satisfies God's wrath. The
Greek verb to propitiate never appears in the
New Testament except in the middle voice,
which indicates that he who is to be propitiated
propitiates himself.[1] In pagan theology the
gods are represented as propitiated ; in the New
Testament God is represented as self-propiti-
ated. Whenever in Christian theology He is
represented as propitiated by another, the theology is in so far paganized. He is represented
in the Bible as having wrath, anger, indignation ; the vocabulary is almost exhausted in
endeavoring to set forth the fire and fierceness

[1] So in 1 John iv. 10 and Romans iii. 25, God is said to have
sent forth his Son to be a propitiation. The Father is Himself the source and origin of this propitiating.

124 AN EVOLUTIONIST'S THEOLOGY

of this wrath. But it is never intimated that
this wrath is appeased or satisfied or propitiated
by another; He appeases it, satisfies it, propitiates it Himself. He is His own propitiator.

If one asks, How can one propitiate himself?
I may reply by the question, How can one be
propitiated in any other way? We are continually going through this double experience of
wrath, anger, indignation, wrong, and the experience of appeasing, propitiating, satisfying
it by our own forthputtings to cure it. This
is a common experience.

A little child falls into a cesspool and comes
crying into the house, the filth dripping from
every part of his garments. The first feeling
of the mother is a feeling of revulsion; and the
more sensitive she is, the greater is her feeling
of revulsion. If she is a half-educated mother,
she first gives the boy a box on the ear by way
of satisfying her wrath. But if she be a truly
refined mother, she takes the child and begins
to cleanse him; and in the very process of
stripping off the garments and putting him
in the bath and washing him and bringing
him out clean and pure, she overcomes, she
satisfies, she appeases, she utilizes her very
wrath against the filth. If she did not have
any such wrath she would not touch the child.
You can see the proof of this every day. You

may see in the tenement house the child with
the filthy face. The mother does not cleanse
him because she does not mind filth; and you
do not cleanse him because the child is not
your child. You must have the two, the love
for the child and the hate of the filth; then
there comes the soap and the water.

And it is in the process of the cleansing that
the revulsion is — not cured, but satisfied. In
the very process of the cleansing, the wrath,
indignation, revulsion, does its work. There is
no righteous wrath which is not a redeeming,
a cleansing, a purifying wrath; and there is no
satisfying of it except as love is so joined to
wrath that the wrath and the love unite in the
process of purification.

Must not God's justice be satisfied? Yes.
But justice is never satisfied by punishment;
certainly not by punishment inflicted on an
innocent person. Vengeance does not satisfy.
It sometimes gluts, but it does not satisfy. The
duelist, angered by insult or wrong, challenges
his enemy to a duel, runs his sword through
the body of his opponent, leaves the life-blood
oozing out of his arteries, wipes his sword, and
walks off in the brightness of the morning.
Satisfied? Never! Nemesis follows him; the
vision is ever before his eyes; he has taken
his vengeance, and the vengeance itself nestles

in his heart and breeds future penalty. Even
if for a little while he is able to forget that
morning, — that ghastly corpse and that oozing
blood, — it will come back to him by and by,
to torture him; for vengeance does not satisfy.
Arrest the burglar, try him, put him in state
prison; are you satisfied? The errand-boy has
robbed the mail; the employer catches him,
brings him before the police magistrate, has
him tried, sentenced to Sing Sing, and dismisses
him. He punishes him, forgets him, blots the
page out of his memory; but he is not satisfied. Another employer, in like circumstances,
says, What can I do for that boy? I must
not let him go; he will become yet worse. He
studies the problem; has the boy committed to
the Elmira Reformatory; when he is reformed,
takes him back, finds a place for him, starts
him on the path of honesty. That is the man
who is satisfied, — the man who appeases his
sense of justice by redeeming the boy from the
wrong in which he was enmeshed. That is what
God is doing. For that Christ came into the
world.

There are many in the Church of Christ
who think of God as a just and punitive God,
who must be satisfied either by penalty laid on
the guilty, or by an equivalent for the penalty.
That is one form of paganism. There are many

who, reacting against that conception, think of
God as an indifferent, careless God, who does
not care much about iniquity, does not trouble
Himself about it, is not disturbed by it! That
is another form of paganism. And there are
many who try to solve the problem by thinking
of two Gods, a just God and a merciful God,
and imagining that the merciful God by the
sacrifice of Himself appeases the wrath of the
just God. That also is a modified form of
paganism. The one transcendent truth which
distinguishes Christianity from all forms of paganism is that it represents God as appeasing
His own wrath or satisfying His own justice by
the forthputting of His own love.[1] But He saves
men from their sins by an experience which we
can interpret to ourselves only by calling it a
struggle between the sentiments of justice and
pity.

Thus the hypothesis of evolution appears
to me to interpret and illumine the doctrine of
redemption as stated in the Bible, and the fact
of redemption as experienced in life. There
is no redemption without this threefold struggle : first, by the soul itself acquiring virtue in

---

[1] It does not come within the scope of this volume to consider in detail the teaching of either Old Testament or New
Testament on this subject. That must be left for the future
volumes of this series on The Bible treated from the evolutionist's point of view. See Preface.

and by the very conflict with temptation ; second, by some higher being, preëminently by God Himself, laying down His own life that He may impart it to others ; and lastly, struggle in the redeeming Spirit, whether human or divine, a struggle between justice and pity, out of which emerges that mercy which satisfies justice by curing the wrong which has aroused the wrath.

CHAPTER IX

EVOLUTION AND MIRACLES

ARE miracles consistent with the doctrine of evolution? This is the question I propose to consider in this chapter. It is no part of my purpose to show that the miracles recorded in the Bible actually took place; only to consider whether belief that they took place is inconsistent with belief in evolution as " God's way of doing things." In fact, I believe that some of the events there recorded, and generally regarded as miraculous, did take place; that others there recorded or referred to did not take place; and concerning others there recorded I am by no means certain whether they took place as recorded, or not. I believe in the resurrection of Jesus Christ as the best attested fact of ancient history; I do not believe that the sun stood still and the moon stayed in the valley of Ajalon at Joshua's command; and I am uncertain as to what interpretation is to be given to the wonderful stories in the Book of Daniel, — whether they are to be regarded as Dean

Farrar regards them, as "lofty moral fiction," or as essentially historical, or as partly imaginative and partly historical. It is proper, however, to say that in my judgment our hypotheses must always be conformed to attested facts ; we must not determine whether we will accept the evidence as to facts by considering whether they agree with our preconceived hypothesis. If I were convinced, for example, that the resurrection of Jesus Christ is not consistent with the doctrine of evolution, I should be compelled to abandon or modify that doctrine ; I should not abandon my belief in the resurrection. That resurrection I regard as a *fact ;* evolution as a theory, — on the whole, the best theory of " God's way of doing things " yet proposed by philosophic thinkers, — the latest word and the best word of science, but not necessarily its last or final word. This may seem to be a digression, but if so it is a necessary digression, — necessary to enable the reader to understand the purpose with which this chapter is written and the point of view of the writer.

Are miracles consistent with the hypothesis of evolution ? To answer this question we must first clearly understand what is a miracle.

The word miracle is a translation — or rather a transliteration — of the Latin word *miraculum,* meaning marvel. This word was used in the fourth century, in the Vulgate or Latin translation of the Bible, to translate a Greek word which should have been translated *signum* or *sign*. Superstition had already entered the Church to misinterpret the Scriptures and degrade primitive Christianity, and the influence of this degradation is seen in the translation in the fourth century of a Greek word meaning *sign* by a Latin word meaning *marvel*. The Greek word meaning marvel (*thauma*) is never used in the New Testament to designate what we now call miracles. They are never regarded as mere marvels. The very word miracle is a verbal infelicity, — an inheritance from a corrupt epoch, bringing with it a corruption of Christian simplicity.

There are in the original Greek New Testament four words used by the sacred writers to designate the supernatural events which we now infelicitously call miracles. They are respectively rendered " wonder," " work," " power," and " sign." But the word " wonder " itself imperfectly represents the original Greek word so translated, for that word signifies not so much an event exciting wonder as an event attracting attention. Moreover, as if the inspired writers feared exactly what has taken place, — the substitution of an appeal to mere marvelousness or wonder for the appeal to the truth signified by the sign, — the word rendered *wonder* is very rarely used except in combination with the word *sign*, as in the familiar phrase, " signs and wonders." Our first answer, then, to the question, What is a miracle? is that it is not a mere marvel. The New Testament knows nothing of thaumaturgy except to condemn it as superstition. It never treats a marvel as a miracle. It never confounds reverence for a truth or a person with astonishment at an event. If Professor Huxley had considered these simple facts, he possibly never would have written his " Essay on the Value of Witnesses to the Miraculous," in which he confounds marvels and the New Testament miracles, which from the New Testament point of view have nothing in common. If our English version had been first translated from the Greek into the English without the intervention of the Vulgate, the word miracle would probably never have appeared in our language to puzzle some and befog others. Dropping, then, for the moment this infelicitous word, and going back to the New Testament writings, we find used in them to designate those extraordinary events which we are now accustomed to designate by the word miracle, these four words, " wonder," " work," " power," and " sign." We may safely assume that any event which fulfills

the meaning of these four words is a miracle
within the meaning of the sacred writers ; and
we may perhaps safely add that no event is a
miracle unless it does fulfill their fourfold meaning.

Such an event must be a *wonder*, — that is,
an event compelling attention by awakening
surprise and exciting at least the spirit of in-
quiry, as the burning bush compelled the attention of Moses, and led him to say, " I will now
turn aside and see this great sight, why the bush
is not burnt." It must be a *work*, — that is, an
achievement, the accomplishment of some beneficent purpose. The devil calls on Jesus to cast
Himself down from the pinnacle of the Temple,
for God will bear Him up so that He will not
dash His foot against a stone ; thus all the people will see His divinity and be conquered by
the wonder. Jesus Christ refuses. This would
be a marvel, but it would not be a work, and the
signs of His divinity must all lie in the achievement of worthy ends. It must be a *power*, —
that is, it must indicate a power more than
human ; thus, when the paralytic is healed,
the people " glorified God, saying, We never
saw it on this fashion," or, on another occasion,
witnessing the healing of the sick by Jesus,
they perceived " the power of Jehovah was
present to heal them." Finally, it must be

a *sign*, that is, the indication or attestation of a divine message or messenger. So Caiaphas says, " This man doeth many *signs ;* if we let Him thus alone, all men will believe on Him." Following this clue in our endeavor to ascertain what the New Testament writers mean us to understand are the distinguishing characteristics of the events which we call miracles, — but which they never call so, — we shall not be far astray if we combine these four words and define the events as follows : An event compelling attention and awakening *wonder*, indicating superhuman *power*, accomplishing some practical *work*, — generally, at least in the New Testament, beneficent in its character, — and furnishing a *sign* of a divine message or messenger.

If this definition is correct, we may dismiss at once such assertions as that of Renan, " Jesus had to choose between these two alternatives, either to renounce His mission or to become a wonder-worker," or that of Professor Huxley : " Jesus is exhibited (in the Second Gospel) as a wonder-worker and exorcist of the first rank." [1] Wonder-worker was exactly what Jesus was not, and constantly refused to be. He was continually appealed to, to work wonders in attestation of His mission, and as constantly declined.

[1] Renan's *Life of Jesus*, chapter xvi., " Science and Christian Tradition ; " Huxley's *Essays*, Preface, p. xxiii,

When His sympathy was appealed to, and by His superhuman power He could do a deed of mercy, as by the healing of the paralytic, the cure of the leper or the blind, or the raising of the dead, He would not refuse. He did not decline to give men help because the help given would excite wonder, but He did invariably refuse to perform works for the sake of exciting wonder. With the possible exception of the story of the money found in the fish's mouth by Peter at Jesus's direction, — a story for that very reason to be regarded with doubt, — every so-called miracle was a use of His power in a work of love. It did excite wonder, and it became a sign of His mission; but it was never done to excite wonder, and it may be boldly affirmed that it would have been no true sign of His mission if it had been wrought for the ignoble purpose of exciting wonder. We may for the same reason dismiss summarily such stories of ecclesiastical miracles as those which Professor Huxley has gathered and rehearsed in the Essay above referred to. Marvels they doubtless are; but they are neither *works* nor *signs*. There is no parallel between them and the New Testament so-called miracles, except that both are unusual events. Professor Huxley narrates as an illustration of an ecclesiastical miracle the story of Eginhard, about A. D. 830, who, about to remove

certain sacred relics from a chest unworthy of
so great a treasure, beheld this "stupendous
miracle, worthy of all admiration. For, just as
when it is going to rain, pillars and slabs and
marble images exude moisture, and, as it were,
sweat, so the chest which contained the most
sacred relics was found moist with blood exud-
ing on all sides." A marvel this certainly was,
but it had no other characteristic of a New
Testament so-called miracle ; it was not a *work*,
for it accomplished nothing, nor a *sign* of superhuman power, for it indicated nothing. It was
simply a marvel, nothing more. Whether we
believe or disbelieve it is morally wholly immaterial ; it attests no truth.

Certain events in the Old Testament which
have been regarded as miracles fall into the
same category of mere marvels. The reason
for believing that the story of Jonah and the
great fish is a satirical fiction, not a history, is
partly its literary structure ; it is also partly the
nature of the marvel related. Marvel the swal-
lowing and preservation of the prophet certainly
is ; but miracle in the New Testament sense it
as certainly is not. For it was not a sign : not
to the sailors, for they knew nothing of it ; not
to the people of Nineveh, for they knew nothing
of it ; not to Jonah, for he needed no sign of
Jehovah's presence and power, having already

confessed both in asking the sailors to cast him into the sea. No mere marvel is a miracle in the New Testament sense of that term. Nothing is such a miracle unless it is a beneficent work, and one which constitutes a sign of a divine truth or person. The question, then, I repeat, is this: Is belief that God has thus attested a divine message or messenger by remarkable works of love and power inconsistent with evolution? that is, with the belief that His way of doing things is the way of working from within outward and in accordance with regular laws, not the way of working from without mechanically and by successive interventions?

That belief in the miracles is inconsistent with the notion that "God created amœbæ, and amœbæ did the rest," is plain enough; but then, no intelligent and honest reader can really suppose that this is what the Christian evolutionist means by evolution; and it would hardly seem that any one familiar with the English language in its modern uses could suppose that this is what any modern writer means by evolution. It ought not to be necessary — to honest and careful readers it is not necessary — to restate my theistic faith. But it may be necessary to repeat here what has been said before, in order to avoid possible misapprehension. The Christian evolutionist believes that God is the one universal and always present Cause; that there are no secondary causes, and that God's method of manifesting His eternal presence is the method of growth, not of manufacture, by a power dwelling within nature and working outward, not by a power dwelling without and working upon nature. Belief in miracles is belief that there have been in history certain wonderful works of love which have attested the divine presence; belief in evolution is belief that growth is "God's way of doing things." Are these two beliefs inconsistent?

In considering this question I start with Herbert Spencer's axiom that "we are ever in the presence of an Infinite and Eternal Energy from which all things proceed." This Energy is personal; not *It*, but *He;* an Energy with individual consciousness; an Energy which thinks, feels, wills. He transcends all phenomena, but dwells in them and manifests Himself through them. He is a Word, ever manifesting Himself; never from eternity has He been a Brahma, dwelling in unconsciousness,— always a Jehovah, putting forth His power in self-manifestations. Not at some remote creative period did He thus manifest Himself in Nature, creating forces then and leaving them to operate automatically thereafter; all forces

are the one Eternal Force ; all days are creative
days ; all growth has the secret of its process in
His perpetual presence. In this self-manifestation He has brought into life moral beings,
like Himself in this, that they also think, feel,
will ; like Himself, therefore, in possessing personality, consciousness, freedom, and, therefore,
moral character. In these men, His children,
formed by Him, but by processes of growth, not
by processes of manufacture, out of preëxisting
forms by His indwelling, not out of dead and
undivine things by external handiwork, He has
further revealed Himself. He has in their consciousness spoken, in their reason inspired His
thoughts, in their hearts His love, in their will
His purpose. He has done this preëminently
in one chosen race, and in that race preëminently in chosen prophets. Why He chose them
it is needless here to inquire. Perhaps because
He chose them, and for no other reason whatever, — so says the Calvinist; perhaps because
He foresaw in them adaptation to be recipients
of His higher life and revelators of it to their
brethren, — so says the Arminian. At length,
when the fullness of time came, He who had
spoken in men, and revealed Himself through
men in fragmentary ways and in divers manners, enters one chosen Man, fills Him full of
Himself, dwells in Him, and through this Man,

Christ Jesus, carries still further that manifestation of Himself for which through the ages He had been preparing, and from which, by the same power of indwelling, He will carry on this self-manifestation until it is completed in a race of men worthy to be called the children of God; that is, a race who in all their characteristics have evidently, unmistakably, unquestionably, not merely been *made* by Him, but have *proceeded* from Him, so that they are in very truth partakers of His nature, companions of His life, manifestations of His character.

Is there anything in this conception of life as a continuous, consistent manifestation of God, all of it proceeding from Him, all of it having for its object a manifestation of Him, and all of it proceeding in a normal and regular manner along the line of cause and effect, — is there anything in this inconsistent with belief that in the life of the Divine Man there were unusual manifestations of the Eternal Power, such as arrested attention then, and served then and since as a sign of the eternal truth that God is in His world working out its redemption?

The opinion that a miracle is a violation of the laws of nature is inconsistent with evolution; the opinion that there have ever been any manifestations of God is inconsistent with atheistic evolution. But the opinion that God has mani-

fested Himself in unusual ways is not inconsistent with belief that He is always manifesting
Himself in all conceivable ways in the ordinary
processes of life.[1]

For let it be remembered again that a miracle
is not a manifestation of an unusual power, but
an unusual manifestation of a continuous power.
It is sometimes said that all nature is a miracle.
If a miracle is simply a sign of superhuman
power, that is true. There is really no greater

---

[1] It has been said that this view "belittles miracles." It
should therefore be said, for the benefit of the non-scholastic
reader, that there is nothing new in it. It is as old as Augustine. "We say that all portents are contrary to nature ; but
they are not so. For how is that contrary to nature which
happens by the will of God ? since the will of so mighty a Creator is certainly the nature of each created thing. A portent,
therefore, happens not contrary to nature, but contrary to
what we know as nature." — Augustine : *The City of God*,
Book XXI. chap. viii. p. 459.

"But I call that a miracle, whatever appears that is difficult or unusual above the hope or power of them who wonder." — *On the Profit of Believing*, § 34, p. 364.

"Since men, intent on a different matter, have lost the consideration of the works of God, by which they should daily
praise Him as the Creator, God has, as it were, reserved to Himself the doing of certain extraordinary actions, that by striking them with wonder He might rouse men as from sleep to
worship Him. A dead man has risen again ; men marvel : so
many are born daily, and none marvels. If we reflect more
considerately, it is a matter of greater wonder for one to be
who was not before, than for one who was to come to life
again." — *On the Gospel of St. John*, Tractate VIII. chap. i.

manifestation of God in the multiplication of
five loaves and two small fishes into food sufficient to feed five thousand than in the multiplication of a bushel of seed-corn into a hundred
bushels ; no greater revelation of His life-giving
power in a resurrection than in a birth. The
only difference between the two is that one is
common, and the other uncommon. And this
answers the question which Renan asks, Why
are not miracles repeated ? The reply is, If they
were repeated they would cease to be miracles.
A miracle constantly repeated becomes a process
of nature. What distinguishes a miracle from
a process of nature is simply that it is not repeated ; it is extraordinary, and for that reason
attracts attention. If resurrection from the dead
were as common as awaking from sleep, we
should think as little of it. The chief reason
why modern thinkers find it difficult to believe
in what we call miracles is either because we
have blindly accepted the too common definition
of miracles as a violation of the laws of nature,
or because we have confounded them with mere
marvels and wonders, or because we have thought
of God as an absentee God, and the miracle as
the token of an exceptional presence. The doctrine of evolution understood as a doctrine of
Divine Immanence, the conception of life as a
continuous and uninterrupted manifestation of

God, will remove these philosophical objections to the miraculous conceived as unusual manifestations of Him. When we believe that all phenomena are directed to a spiritual purpose, and that the object of all life is to manifest the Eternal Presence, we shall not be surprised to find in history special manifestations of that Presence in order to serve that spiritual purpose.

For evolution does not teach that the processes of what we call nature cannot be brought under spiritual control. On the contrary, it shows their operation under the spiritual control of man, guided and directed to a definite purpose by human intelligence and human will. Evolution is carried on by what we call natural selection up to the point when man appears upon the scene; then man himself begins to direct, control, modify, regulate, evolution. He shapes it as he will; his intelligence masters it and directs it. He determines whether the soil shall produce a rose or a lily, an oak or an elm. He finds a prairie strewed with grass and wild flowers, and out of that same prairie he evolves this year a cornfield, next year a wheatfield. Early travelers tell us of a great American desert, apparently useless to man, which extended from the Missouri River to the Rocky Mountains. It has now become a fertile and prosperous region. Man has made this former wilderness to

bud and blossom as a rose. He has used the
forces of nature, has conformed to the laws of
nature, and thus has regulated the evolutionary
processes of nature. In thus directing them to
a predetermined end, he follows in the footsteps
of One greater than he is. The charcoal-burn-
ers in the mountains, who fell the trees and burn
them in a furnace in which very little oxygen is
admitted, are simply imitating on a small scale
what in the far-off centuries God did when He
turned the great trees of the carboniferous era
into coal. Out of this coal formerly men distilled the illuminating oil. They did but repeat
what God had done in the former ages when He
filled the subterranean reservoirs with a like
material by a similar process. Our dynamo —
a magnetic wheel revolving with great rapidity
in a magnetic field — imitates God's dynamo;
for now we know that this globe on which we
live is itself a great magnet, and is itself revolving in a magnetic field. The growths of
the past have been under the supervision of a
controlling will, directed by intelligence to benevolent ends. The processes of nature and of
civilization combine to demonstrate beyond all
question that matter is subordinate to spirit. If
by nature is meant the physical realm, then the
supernatural is not only about us, but within us.
The whole fabric of modern civilization is based

upon this : that matter is controlled by that which is superior to matter ; that spirit can direct, control, manipulate, physical forces.

Why, then, should we think it an extraordinary thing that the Father, " of whom the whole family in heaven and earth is named," should accompany the two great messages the human race needs with some token of His presence such as the blindest could not fail to see? What does man need, what does America need, more than these two words, Law and Love? The voice of conscience within us echoes the voice of a divine authority without. The world needed some attestation of that in the beginning. Once attested, once recognized, it has gone on growing in human consciousness until the laws of conscience are recognized as the laws of God. And that other message, — that when men have violated God's law, there is a power not ourselves that makes for righteousness, — why should we think it strange that the Father should give that message, and should accompany it with attestations of His presence and His power such as made the world stop and listen ?

If we approach the question of miracles from the point of view of a pure physicist, we shall in the first place be inclined to disbelieve in them, and in the second place not much care whether they occurred or not. With a phenomenon occurring but once, and never since repeated, science does not concern itself. But what Campbell Fraser has put as a question we may transform into affirmation : " The physical miracle finds its natural significance in its *moral* relations to the *persons* in the universe, rather than in its physical relations to the things in the universe." The miracle is an unusual witness to Him whose presence is constantly witnessed, but, because the witness is constant, is too often ignored.

The doctrine of evolution, then, is not, as it seems to me, inconsistent with belief that at certain epochs in the world's history, and for certain special moral ends, there occurred unusual events which awakened attention and have served as signs of a superhuman power wrought in works either of judgment or mercy, although almost uniformly the latter. And this conviction, it is proper to add, I share with evolutionists who on other grounds absolutely reject the miraculous. " It is not," says Professor Huxley, " upon any *a priori* considerations that objections either to the supposed efficacy of prayer or to the supposed occurrences of miracles can be based, and to my mind the fatal objection to both these suppositions is the inadequacy of the evidence to prove any given case of such occurrence which has been adduced." The question whether God answers prayer, the question whether the so-called miracles or any of them recorded in the Bible ever took place, are to be determined by evidence simply. If the evidence sustains the affirmative answer, there is nothing in evolution inconsistent with that answer.

CHAPTER X

A MIRACLE — that is, an extraordinary event arresting attention and awakening *wonder*, accomplishing some beneficent *work*, and by its manifestation of a superhuman *power* serving as a *sign* of a divine message or messenger — may either be in accordance with human experience or may transcend human experience. The first is as truly a miracle as the second ; what constitutes it a miracle is not that it is an event out of the ordinary course of nature, but that it serves effectually as a sign of superhuman power in the accomplishment of a moral end. The two greatest miracles of the Old Testament are not events transcending human experience ; they were wrought by what we customarily call natural forces, and in accordance with what we call natural laws. What made them miracles was such an evident connection with a moral end that they served as signs of the directing presence of a moral Person, possessing superhuman power. The first of these miracles was the destruction of the Cities of the Plain, the second the passage of the Red Sea by the children of Israel.

The desolate region of the Dead Sea is a perpetual attestation of the awful work of destruction wrought there in some early age by a combination of earthquake and volcano. The now extinct volcano furnished the fire and brimstone which Jehovah rained from heaven. The accompanying earthquake was the means by which He overthrew cities which the inhabitants had fondly imagined were built to endure forever. The bitumen with which the soil abounds, set on fire by subterranean heats, made the smoke of the country to go up from the plain as the smoke of a furnace. The fall of saline ashes from the volcano caught and incrusted the belated fugitive and arrested her flight. In the destruction of the Cities of the Plain, narrated in the Book of Genesis, there is nothing more difficult for an evolutionist to believe than in the accounts of the destruction of Lisbon by earthquake as narrated in secular history. Nor is it made more incredible because a sacred writer saw in it a sign of divine judgment on cities wholly given over to infamous wickedness.

The other great miracle of the Old Testament, that which is indelibly connected in Jew-

ish history with the birth of the nation, the
passage of the Red Sea, is distinctly attributed
by the sacred historian to what we call natural
causes. "And Jehovah," he says, "caused the
sea to go back by a strong east wind all that
night, and made the sea dry." The traveler
may to-day pass over the roadway, with marshes
on either side, where once on one side was the
sea, and on the other a shallow bay, and he may
see the dangerous quicksands where Pharaoh's
chariot-wheels dragged heavily. He may thus
see in the topography of the locality a witness
to the scientific probability of the incident so
graphically described by the sacred historian.
So long as high winds and ebbing tides uncover
beaches along the sea, and returning tides and
changing winds re-cover them, so long he will
find nothing in the doctrine of evolution incon-
gruous with the belief that Israel passed over
a ford thus prepared, and that Pharaoh's host,
following, were caught by the returning tide and
overwhelmed in the treacherous sands. There
is nothing, then, in this narrative more difficult
for a scientist to believe than in the account in
our own history of a protecting fog under cover
of which Washington's army escaped after the
battle of Long Island, or in that of the incursion of the sea, in the history of the Netherlands, by which the siege of Leyden was raised

in the days of William the Silent. Whether
these events occurred is, therefore, simply a
question of history. The evidence of the destruction of the Cities of the Plain is to be found
in the aspect of the Dead Sea valley, which bears
witness to a dreadful catastrophe in the remote
past. The evidence of the passage of the Red
Sea is found in a tradition wrought into the history of a great people, repeated in their songs,
celebrated in their great national birthday, and
incidentally confirmed by the physical characteristics of the region, which at once interpret
the account and confirm its accuracy.

The other form of miracle transcends human
experience. It presents to us a phenomenon
unlike any with which we are familiar, and must
either be left unexplained, or explained, if at
all, by hypotheses, not indeed irrational, but
confessedly unproved. Most of the miracles
of the New Testament are of this description.
It is true that there are in the cure of nervous
diseases, and especially in the control and cure
of the insane, by a strong and dominant nature,
some analogies which throw light upon certain
cures wrought by Christ and narrated in the
Gospels. It is true that the triumph of medical
science in restoring life to persons who, according to all the tests we know how to apply, have
appeared to be absolutely dead, suggests a pos-

sible interpretation of some of the cases of resurrection. Yet the great majority of Christ's
miracles, including that which is the most transcendent of them all, His own resurrection from
the dead, transcend all our experiences of life.
All that we can do is, first to try to state them
to ourselves in thinkable forms, and then to
ask whether the evidence is such as to warrant
our belief in them. Within the limits of this
chapter, I can illustrate this method by only
a single instance, that of the resurrection of
Jesus Christ, and can do even this only very
inadequately.

The accounts of His resurrection, as given
in the four Gospels, may here be condensed
into a sentence : Jesus Christ was sentenced to
death ; the priests and Pharisees were present
to make sure that He should not escape their
malice ; had He been taken from the cross before death was assured, the centurion would
have paid the penalty of his neglect with his
own life ; and, finally, the death of the crucified
was demonstrated before the body was taken
from the cross, by the thrust of the spear into
the side. The body was buried in the tomb on
Friday evening. On Sunday morning the disciples came to the tomb, to find it empty : they
were in despair, thinking that the body had
been stolen ; nor was their despair overcome

until after repeated appearances of the risen
Lord to them, singly and in companies. This
is the account. Is it so far consistent with what
we know of God's way of doing things as to
be inherently credible? If so, is it sufficiently
attested by adequate evidence to be credited?
My answer to both these questions is in the
affirmative.

I. What is God's way of doing things, according to evolution? It is to develop life by
successive processes, until a spirit akin to His
appears in a bodily organism akin to that of
the lower animals from which it has been pre-
viously evolved. This bodily organism is from
birth in a state of constant decay and repair.
At length the time comes when, through disease
or old age, the repair no longer keeps pace with
the decay. Then the body returns to the earth,
and the spirit to God who gave it. This dis-
embodying of the spirit we call death. There
is at death an end of the body. It knows no
resurrection save in grass and flowers. The
resurrection, the *anastasis* or up-standing as
the New Testament calls it, is the resurrection
of the spirit. The phrase " resurrection of the
body " never occurs in the New Testament.
But every death is a resurrection of the spirit.
What we call death the New Testament calls
an " exodus " or an emancipation from bondage,

an "unmooring" or setting the ship free from its imprisonment.[1] The spirit is released from its confinement, and this release is death. Death is, in short, not a cessation of existence, not a break in existence; it is simply what Socrates declared it to be, "the separation of the soul and body. And being dead is the attainment of this separation; when the soul exists in herself, and is parted from the body, and the body is parted from the soul, — that is death." [2]

The Christian who holds this view of death and resurrection believes that that occurred to Jesus Christ which occurs to all God's children at death : the spirit was separated from the body to exist in itself. In this general belief in a phenomenon transcending experience there is nothing more inconsistent with evolution than in the belief in the separation of the child from the mother at birth, or in the belief that the grub issues at a certain stage of its existence from its subaqueous life and enters upon a new experience as a dragon-fly. In brief, evolution is not inconsistent with the idea that a living creature in one stage of existence is being prepared for a future stage of existence which will

---

[1] Luke ix. 31, English "decease; " 2 Tim. iv. 6, English "departure."

[2] *Phædo*, Jowett's translation, vol i. p. 390.

entirely transcend the present experience; on the contrary, this is precisely what it teaches us to expect. The only real question in respect to the resurrection of Jesus Christ is not, Is it incredible that the resurrection took place? but, Is it incredible that it was followed by such appearances to the disciples as to bring it within the range of their observation, and afford them tangible evidence that it had taken place? Such an appearance is certainly extraordinary; but it seems to me not at all incredible either that the spirit should have returned to reanimate the body, or that it should have given visible evidence of itself as disembodied, for the very purpose of converting what was in Socrates and Cicero a mere vague expectation into what has become in the Christian Church throughout the ages an assured and certain faith.

II. Assuming that the appearances of Jesus Christ to His disciples after His death are not inherently incredible, are they so attested that we have reason to credit them? An adequate answer to this question cannot be expected to be crowded into a paragraph, when volumes have been written in answering it. I can only say in the briefest terms why I regard those appearances as among the best attested facts of ancient history.

Literary study has demonstrated that three

of the four Gospels were written in less than
half a century after Christ's death; that the
fourth Gospel was written within three quarters
of a century after that death; and that in all
four we have substantially the testimony of
the eye-witnesses themselves, not the product
of a later tradition.   That these eye-witnesses
were not intentional deceivers is now universally
admitted; [1] that they were deceived by Jesus
Christ, as they would have been on the supposi-
tion that He did not really die, but only swooned,
no one will now pretend to affirm; that their
belief was the product of their enthusiastic ex-
pectations of a resurrection, as Renan suggests,
is absolutely inconsistent with all that we know
of these singularly prosaic, unemotional, unim-
aginative characters, and with all that the accounts tell us of their disbelief in the first
reports, and of the frequent appearances necessary to convince them of the fact of the resurrection.

If this, their testimony, stood alone, it would
probably be disregarded by the great majority
of mankind as unimportant, if not incredible.
But it does not stand alone.   It is closely related to the most stupendous changes which
have ever taken place in the life of the world.

---

[1] "Only this much need be acknowledged, that the disciples
firmly believed that Jesus had arisen." — Strauss.

Perhaps the least, although the most immedi-
ately visible of these changes is the institution
of the First Day of the week as one of universal
observance. This day has passed over from
Palestine to Greece, Rome, Continental Europe,
Great Britain, and America. It has survived
changes of government, law, civilization, and
language, as well as of ritual and creed. It
is alike recognized by Roman Catholic, Greek,
Anglican, and Puritan, and is coming to be
recognized by Jews, and demanded as a privi-
lege by unbelievers. This day, which neither
covetousness nor infidelity has been able to abol-
ish, neither superstition nor legalism to destroy, celebrates nothing and is unmeaning
if there was no resurrection of Jesus Christ.
Yet this day is but a symbol of changes vastly
greater. On faith in that resurrection the
Church is itself historically built. Within less
than thirty years after it was supposed to have
taken place, Paul, in his Epistle to the Corinthians, — written, according to the testimony of all
critics, before A. D. 60, — declared to the Christians in pagan Corinth that their Christian faith
was built upon this fact, and that if Christ had
not risen their faith was vain. Not only the
Church, but Christianity as a historical religion,
is founded upon faith in that resurrection.
Christianity is not merely a new or a reformed

ethical system ; it is a message of victory over
sin and death. It has appealed not merely
to the consciences of mankind, but still more
to their love and to their hope. The assurance
of immortality expressed in the Easter song,
" Thanks be to God which giveth us the victory," has appealed to the discouraged and the
despairing, and given them new life. That new
life has borne its fruits in a civilization which
has always been proportioned to the strength of
that faith and hope in a risen Christ. If Christ
did not rise from the dead, the Christian Sunday, the Christian Church, and Christian civilization are founded on a falsehood, on a delusion,
if not on a fraud. Science requires belief in an
intellectual order in the universe. Moral life
requires belief in a moral order in the universe.
To believe that the whole fabric of Christian
civilization is founded on a lie is to believe that
in the moral realm causes have no relation to
the effects which they produce. It is to rele-
gate us to moral chaos.

It will not reasonably be expected that in two
paragraphs in such a volume as this the grounds
of Christian faith in Christ's resurrection can
be adequately stated. All that I have here attempted is to indicate the twofold basis on which
that faith seems to me to rest. That faith assumes that God is, and that God is good ; that

He manifests himself to His children in order
that He may bring His children into fellowship
with Him ; that Christ is the incomparable One
in human history whose life and character furnish a unique manifestation of the Father of all
the living. And, assuming this, Christian faith
believes in the manifestation of Christ to His
disciples after His death as a demonstration
of that resurrection which accompanies every
dying : first, because faithful, honest, and trust-
worthy men have borne witness to such appearances ; and, second, because Christian civilization, the Christian Church, and the Christian
Sunday are living and perpetual witnesses to
such resurrection. Into these two categories
fall the evidences which have led the greatest
statesmen and jurists — men accustomed to sift
and weigh evidence — to accept the visible resurrection of Jesus Christ as one of the best
attested facts of ancient history.

CHAPTER XI

EVOLUTION AND IMMORTALITY

IMMORTALITY does not seem to me to be capable of scientific demonstration. If by immortality we simply mean that those who seem to have died continue to live after death, ghosts, slates, table-tippings, rappings, and such like might, perhaps, afford a scientific demonstration of this not very important fact. But if immortality means a life in the other world that transcends any life in this, a life far beyond any experience here below, a life free from the trammels of the body, a life glorious beyond all imaginings, it is impossible that it should be demonstrated. For such a life lies in the future, and science has to do exclusively with the present and the past. It may anticipate the future, but it can test only what actually is. All that science can do respecting immortality is to look at life from the evolutionary point of view and see what evolution would naturally lead us to anticipate in the future, — death or life. And it appears to me that belief in evolution, so far from weakening faith in immortality, strengthens it, and I might almost say necessitates it.   It does not demonstrate immortality, and yet I do not see how one can be a consistent evolutionist and think that " death ends all."

Let the reader imagine himself looking upon a vast cloud of subtle but visible ether. As he looks, this ether gathers itself together into a globe and begins a revolution gradually increasing in rapidity.   As it revolves, it cools, separates into solid and liquid matter; mists arise from it, and become floating and swimming clouds; mimic mountains are pushed up from its gradually corrugated surface; mimic oceans and seas and lakes and rivers are formed upon it; forests appear, and various verdure, and decorating flowers, and, last of all, moving creatures in air and sea and land.   Something like this science does see.   It sees the great formless chaos gathering itself together into a globe and hanging unsupported in the heavens; it sees through the long ages this globe gradually cooling; it sees the oceans and the seas and the lakes and the rivers forming below; it sees the steam rising into clouds and floating above; it sees the great forests growing, the grass and verdure springing up; it sees the process of storage of coal and iron and copper and gold and

silver in the mountain fastnesses ; it sees the
earth made rich with juices which will feed un-
numbered thousands in the future ; it sees gradually appearing upon this globe animals, —
fishes, reptiles, birds, mammals, and, last of all,
man ; and, looking upon him, it sees him taking possession of this globe.   He is probably,
as an infant, the feeblest of all the infant animals, and even as a full-grown adult he does not
compare in strength with many others.   They
have advantages over him in many respects ;
but he alone possesses reason, conscience, and a
rational and moral will.   In this intellectual
and moral nature he transcends them all, and
by virtue of this intellectual and moral nature
he takes possession of the globe.   He first sees
the use of its stored-up treasures.   He discovers
the light and heat locked up in coal, and re-
leases them.   He discovers the use of iron, con-
verts it into tools, and makes them serve his
purpose in manufacture.   He learns how to
avail himself of the forces of nature, — gravitation, light, electricity, heat.   The animals that
seem to be his superiors are subordinate to
him.   Some he domesticates, others he conquers, all he cows and controls.   He is the
master of the world in which he has been
placed.
    Looking upon this process, beginning with the

nebulous condition in the outset, and tracing it gradually until we come to the present condition, two things seem very clear to the theistic evolutionist. First, that there is a design in this creation. It has been governed by a master will, and guided to a definite and projected end. He perceives that the creative process has gone on by forces, whether from within or without, that were aiming at some ultimate result. He traces the growth of life from the single cell up to the complicated condition of present civilization, and sees that in this development there has been a culmination which has been steadily sought. He is not so certain as the fathers were about designs, but he is more certain than they were about design. He is not so sure about the adaptations of particular things to particular ends, but he is more certain that the whole process of creation, beginning with the world in its nebulous condition and reaching on to the present, has had a definite purpose which has been consistently pursued. In other words, he sees that the " Infinite and Eternal Energy, from which all things proceed," is an intellectual energy which has thought something out ; a purposeful energy which was resolved to accomplish certain results ; a benevolent energy which has been seeking the happiness and welfare of others.

This is the first thing the evolutionist sees ; the second is — Man. Though he may be perplexed in the detail, the evolutionist is sure that the end of this design, the purpose which has been steadily kept in view, is man. Whatever other worlds may be for, whatever the wide universe in its wider scope may be for, this globe on which we dwell has been fashioned, built, constructed, to be the habitation of man. It is man who has taken possession of it; it is man who understands it ; it is man who is using it; it is man who comprehends its laws, who masters its forces, who avails himself of its riches, who dominates all the other creatures upon it. It is not more certain that the cell is made for the storage of the honey by the bee, that the nest is made for the home of the birdling, that the cradle is made for the rocking of the babe, than it is that this globe was made for the habitation and the development of man.

And man is not only the supreme result of evolution thus far, — he is the final result of evolution ; there is nothing beyond him. If one asks, How do we know that there may not be something inconceivable to us beyond? the answer is, We cannot *know ;* but in our attempt to unriddle the enigma of the universe we must think with our faculties and be governed by

our limitations, and we can *conceive* nothing
higher than man. We can conceive of man
infinitely improved ; we can conceive of him
cultivated, developed, enlarged, enriched, purified ; but of anything essentially higher than
man — no. Nothing can be conceived higher
than to think, to will, to love. If we look back
along the pages of history, these two truths we
have learned from the universe : first, that all
its processes have been for the purpose of manifesting One who thinks, who wills, who loves ;
second, that the purpose in the manifestation of
this One is the creation of a race of free moral
agents, who can themselves think and will and
love. The inorganic world existed before the
vegetable, and the vegetable world existed before the animal, and the lower animal existed
before man, but man exists for nothing beyond.
The very topmost round of the ladder has been
reached : to know right from wrong, to do the
right and eschew the wrong, to understand invisible distinctions, to perceive the invisible
world, to struggle toward something higher and
yet higher, and yet always to know, to resolve,
to love, — this is supreme.

And has all been done that thinking and
willing and loving may run their insect course
in a flitting moment of time, and then end ? Is
the whole process of evolution for this, and no-

thing more? Are we to think that this long cycle
of ages has run its course, and chaos has been
converted into order, and out of order the architectural splendor of the heavens and earth has
been fashioned, and in that architectural splendor of the heavens and the earth life has been
developed, first in its lower vegetable forms, and
then in its intermediary animal forms, and
finally out of these the highest conceivable life,
the capacity to think, to feel, to will, only that
thinking, feeling, willing, may continue for
thirty, forty, fifty, or sixty years, and then cease:
ages for a lifetime, an eternity for an instant,
the whole long process of development culmi-
nating in — nothing? When men believed that
God had made by successive creations different
beings; when they believed that He had made
the world by one voice, the vegetable world by
another, the animal world by another, each spe-
cies of animals by a separate voice, and man by
a separate voice, one can understand how then
men might have said, He has made man for his
little day; man will decay, and God will make
others to take his place, — though even then
Tennyson's argument was hard for the heart to
answer : —

> " Thou wilt not leave us in the dust :
>   Thou madest man, he knows not why ;
>   He thinks he was not made to die ;
>   And Thou hast made him : Thou art just."

Even then, if one looked on man and saw how his aspirations and desires reached out into eternity, how he projected himself into eternity, how he set forces to work that were reaching forward into the far future, — even then it were difficult to see why it should be thought that " death ends all." But when one believes that the whole creation is focused on man, — that the whole process of the planetary system, beginning so far back that not memory nor even imagination can conceive it, issues in man ; when one believes that the whole process of the long evolution, purposed in the divine love, thought out in the divine mind, and wrought out by divine energy, has been accomplished for the purpose of producing a thinking, willing, loving man, how is it possible for him to believe that the end of it all is — nothing ?

Let us look at this man a little more closely. He begins in a single cell, and passes through the successive stages of different animals. He is successively reptile, bird, fish, vertebrate mammal, and at last becomes man. I do not speak of the race, but of the individual ; he comes into what we call life through these successive stages of previous lives. He is born, dwelling in a body ; and we do not need the scientist to tell us his subsequent history. That process we easily trace in three successive stages. First, this

body is the necessary means for his development.
He is developed by the body. He learns through
the eye and the ear, the hand and the foot, the
activities of the physical organization. Is he
blind, one element of his development is cut
off; is he deaf, another element; is he deprived
of the sense of touch, a third element. With
these all gone some development may be carried
on, but, speaking generally, it may be said that
the body is necessary to his development. By
the very discipline he receives through his body
his soul is moulded and shaped. He is educated
through the physical organization. Then he
comes into the second stage, in which this body
becomes the necessary instrument of his activity. It is the power by which he operates on
the world without. His lungs, his heart, his
stomach, keep the machine in order, while the
machine is being used to impart to other lives.
Because he has hands which are themselves tools,
he makes tools, as no handless animal can. Because he has eyes, he can produce color, which
otherwise he could not produce. With his
tongue he speaks, and communicates his thoughts
to others. With his pen he writes, and communicates his life to other lives. His body is the
necessary instrument of his activity, — this is the
second stage. Finally, in old age, he comes into
the third stage, in which the body becomes a

hindrance to his development. He still has the
same power to perceive truth that he always had,
but he has become deaf and cannot hear. He
has the same artistic sense that he always had,
but he has become blind and cannot see. He
has the same burning thoughts with which he
was wont to inspire audiences, but his voice has
lost its music and its power; he cannot reach
the audience. He is still a musician, and the
music is in his soul, but the voice is gone; we
want to hear him sing no more. His very brain
ceases to formulate thought. His soul has outgrown the body. First it was the instrument
for development; second, an instrument for use-
fulness; now it is neither. He has not grown
old, but the organ that he used has grown old.
Gladstone is not old. Put him in a new body,
— what a magnificent statesman he would be!
Henry Ward Beecher was not old. Bring him
back and put him in a body forty years old, —
how his eloquence would again stir the heart of
the nation! Men do not grow old; it is the body
which grows old, unable to fulfill its function as
the servant of the spirit.

All through its appointed threescore years
and ten the body is dying, — from the very
cradle dying; constantly used up, constantly re-
paired. That has been the history year after
year, until at last the repair can no longer make

up for the ravages of time, because the soul has outgrown the body. What then? Remember, from the first nebulous days God had in mind a man. Through all the long cycles of geology, through all the cycles of prehistoric history, through all the creative days of the past, through all the later creative days, through family, through various forms of government, through justice and injustice, through war and peace, through commerce, education, and religion, He has been making *men*. And every man He has put into a body, that at first helped to development, and then helped to service, and then became a hindrance to development and a hindrance to service, because the soul had outgrown the body. What then? Why, if there is not something that lies beyond when the body is gone, all evolution ends in a *cul-de-sac*. It is inconceivable that God should have spent all the ages in making a Gladstone, a Lincoln, a Jefferson, a Shakespeare, only that He might make a body with which to fill a grave.

There are two alternatives: that of positivism and that of pantheism. The positivist tells us: Yes, there is an immortality, but it is an immortality of influence. Shakespeare is immortal: his plays will live. Plato is immortal: his thoughts will inspire men through all coming ages. Lincoln is immortal: his courage and his heroism will make heroes to all future time. The immortality is an immortality of influence, and it is for future generations that present generations live. But what is the use of future generations? Why is there a Shakespeare, a Bacon, a Gladstone, a Jefferson, a Hamilton, a Washington, a Lincoln? Only to make insects that dance for an hour in the sunbeam, and then are gone? I can understand the evolutionist who does not believe in universal immortality, who thinks only the fittest will survive. I can even comprehend the belief that this present race of men is not worthy to live immortally, that this present race of men will perish, but by and by, when God's providence has worked out its culmination, there will come from them a race that will live immortally, and we are but preparing for them. But I cannot understand how a consistent evolutionist can believe that "death ends all;" that throughout all these ages God has been preparing men such as men are, only to make other men such as these men are, all to fill one great cemetery at the end. As John Fiske says, "God is not like a child that builds a house of cards to blow it down again." [1]

---

[1] Dr. Newman Smyth, in a volume published as this volume is undergoing the last preparation for the press, shows from a scientific point of view that death is not the end of life, but life is the end of death. "Man himself might not have been made of the dust of the earth, if that dust had not been

The other conception is pantheistic. It is the old Hindu conception, repeated in modern theosophy. All things will run their circuit and come back to God Himself. *Man* is immortal, but men are not personally immortal. The sun draws the water from the ocean, shapes it in a cloud, hangs it in the heavens, drops it upon the hills; it falls into the spring and the river, and so flows back again into the ocean. Thus God sends out souls, that, after they have traveled the circuit of their being, they may return to Him again. Such is the pantheistic conception. Are we, then, to think that God has been working through the ages for nothing; that the end of all His work is simply that He is just where He was before; that He has struck some sparks out of His heart, which have floated a little while in the universe, and then come back into His heart again; that He has lived for naught; that evolution has traveled its circuit, and come back to the cradle from whence it issued? Nay, more than that; for if this were true, God would not be God. For God is *love*, and you cannot love if there is not some one to love; and if God is all, and all things come back to

mingled of the elements of the dead forms which were before him. We owe our human birth to death in nature. The earth before us has died that we might live. We are the living children of a world that has died for us." — Dr. Newman Smyth: *The Place of Death in Evolution*, p. 31

God, — if, as all drops of water return to the great ocean, so all individual souls come back to be absorbed in Him again, — there is no one to love, and God is the loveless one. If "death ends all," either He is a Father who watches an eternal funeral, and all the music of the spheres is but as the music of muffled drums, and the end of all the travail of His soul is death, or else He is a God who does not love, did not love, cannot love, because there are none whom He may love.

Over against these conceptions I place that of the Christian evolutionist, expressed in the words of Paul, — "The earnest expectation of the creature waiteth for the manifestation of the sons of God." Through all these ages God has been working out something that was worth working out. He has been developing through all these ages sons of God ; creatures that could think as He thinks, will as He wills, love as He loves, and carry their independence and their personality into a future life to love and be loved. As we have seen, according to evolution the creation has always been looking forward to something higher and better. This is that earnest expectation of the creation which Paul interprets. Immortality is not a demonstrated fact, but it is a necessary anticipation. Without it all evolution would be meaningless.

The figures of the poets are not merely figures; they are scientific prophecies. When the integument of the seed ceases to serve the purpose of the seed and keeps the life from growing, the seed becomes a corpse, and out of the dead body there issues the new life. When the egg ceases to be any longer a protection to the bird, and if it were kept intact would become a prison-house, forbidding further development, it is broken, and the bird comes out. When the chrysalis is no longer a protection to the grub, the chrysalis is sloughed off, and the butterfly issues. Man himself was once an egg. Man himself once dwelt in a prison-house of absolute darkness, like the seed in the ground. If he has come from the egg into manhood, from the dark imprisonment into the light of life, it would be strange, when the body has ceased to fulfill its function, has ceased to be the instrument of life, if he did not cast it off, bury it forever, have no more of it, and rise triumphant to the larger life for which all the evolutionary processes of the centuries have been preparing him.

More than the ancient conception of creation as an instantaneous process, evolution, as the interpretation of creation, looks forward to a life beyond the grave, and cries with a loud Amen, like the four living creatures in the

Book of Revelation, to the prophetic declaration, " The earnest expectation of the creature waiteth for the manifestation of the sons of God."

CHAPTER XII

A SUMMARY OF CONCLUSIONS

In this chapter I propose to give a brief review of the preceding chapters, and to sum up the conclusions therein reached.

Evolution is not to be identified with Darwinism; it is not the doctrine of struggle for existence and the survival of the fittest. Evolution is, broadly speaking, the doctrine of growth applied to life; the doctrine that life is a growth; the doctrine that all life proceeds by natural and normal processes from lower to higher stages, from simpler to more complex stages, and by a vital force or forces operating from without.

Evolution does not attempt to explain the origin of life. It is simply a history of the process of life. With the secret cause of life evolution has nothing to do. A man, therefore, may be a materialistic evolutionist or a theistic evolutionist; that is, he may believe that the cause is some single unintelligent, impersonal force, or he may believe that the cause

is a wise and beneficent personal God. I repeat
what I have already said in this volume, that
I am a theistic evolutionist; that is, I believe
that the Infinite and Eternal Energy from
which all things proceed, which is the All in
all, is an Energy that thinks, feels, and wills,
— a self-conscious, intelligent, moral Being.

Evolution does not claim to be the last word.
There is no last word. Evolution itself is inconsistent with the idea that there can be any
last word. The doctrine of evolution is the
doctrine of perpetual growth, and therefore
every word spoken prepares for another and a
further word. If it is to be accepted at all,
it is to be accepted as, on the whole, the grand-
est generalization of our age, if not of any age,
— the best statement of the process of life that
has yet been uttered.

All biologists accept evolution; practically,
all natural scientists accept evolution. Le
Conte says, " I think truly that you might as
well speak of a gravitationist as of an evolutionist." But that is not all. Evolution is to-day
accepted as the clue in their investigations by
all teachers, in all departments, in all colleges
and institutions of learning, except possibly
in the department of theology. History, political economy, literature, and moral philosophy,
no less than the various natural sciences, are

treated from the evolutionary point of view
and according to the principles of evolutionary
philosophy. In our colleges and higher institutions of learning, of every description, male and
female, orthodox and unorthodox, the courses
of education are founded on the assumption
that the history of life is a history of growth
from lower to higher forms, from simpler to
more complex forms, according to laws that are
comprehensible, and by forces resident within
the phenomena themselves. In this condition
of learning there are three courses which the
religious teacher may take. The first course
is for him to set himself in antagonism to evolution. He may enter upon the biological field ;
he may point out gaps here and there in the
process, and may show that evolution does not
explain everything : and thus he may satisfy
himself, and perhaps those of his congregation
who have not studied the subject, that the hypothesis of evolution is untrue ; but it must be
frankly said, he will satisfy no one else. When
the whole scientific and intellectual world is
moving in one direction, the minister who is not
a scientific expert may get himself run over,
but he cannot stop the procession by getting in
front of it. The second course is for the religious teacher to maintain that there is a difference between the spiritual realm and the natural

realm.   Conceding that it is true that evolution is the law of the natural realm, he may insist that there is some other law which operates in the spiritual realm, or at all events that the law of growth does not operate with uniformity. Conceding that there are no interferences, no breaks, in the continuity of cause and effect in nature, he may insist that there are interventions in the continuity of cause and effect in the moral and spiritual realm.   There is some reason for thus differentiating the moral and the material realms ; one may do this and be rational and self-consistent.   And yet it seems to me that, if we believe that there is one God — God of the physical and material nature, God of the spiritual and intellectual nature — we shall be more and more inclined to believe that His method of work in the world is one; that He does not proceed in the two realms by methods which are themselves inconsistent.   The third course is for the religious teacher frankly to accept evolution ; to say to the scientist, Since you have studied this subject and this is your verdict, I accept it, and I will see what light is thrown upon the problems of the moral life. In so doing, he seems to me to have the authority of the Master.   " And He [Jesus] said, So is the kingdom of God, as if a man should cast seed into the ground ; and should sleep, and rise

night and day, and the seed should spring and
grow up, he knoweth not how. For the earth
bringeth forth fruit of herself; first the blade,
then the ear, after that the full corn in the
ear." [1] In this parable Christ not only implies
that there is a true analogy between " God's
way of doing things " in the spiritual and in the
material realm, but He anticipates Le Conte's
definition of evolution, and applies its three
principles to the spiritual realm : first, " continuous progressive change," — first the blade, then
the ear, then the full corn in the ear ; second,
" according to certain laws," — it springs and
grows up ; third, " by means of resident forces,"
— the earth bringeth forth fruit of herself.

I believe, then, that the great laws of life
which natural science has elucidated from a
study of natural phenomena are analogous to, if
not identical with, the laws of the spiritual life,
and that the latter are to be interpreted by the
former. The object of this book is to afford
some aid to the perplexed by throwing upon
the mystery of the spiritual life the light which
the philosophy of evolution has already thrown
upon the material life. This may revolutionize
theology, but it will strengthen and enrich religious faith. For there is a great difference
between theology and religion. Religion is a

[1] Mark iv. 26–28.

spiritual life; theology is the science of that
life. It is very important that we should have
a correct science of life, but it is also very important that we should understand that the science is not the life. The life remains essentially
unchanged through centuries, but the science
is continually changing. The religious life of
faith and hope and love is, in its essential elements, what it was when Abraham turned his
back upon idolatry that he might go out in
quest of the true God; but the theology of the
most conservative orthodox church in America
is very different from the theology of Abraham.
What is religion? If we ask the Bible for definitions, we shall find such as this: " What doth
the Lord require of thee, but to do justly, and to
love mercy, and to walk humbly with thy God?"
Then religion is justice, mercy, humility. Or
such as this: " The grace of God . . . hath
appeared . . . teaching us that . . . we should
live soberly, righteously, and godly in this present world, looking for . . . the glorious appearing of the great God and our Saviour." Then
religion is sobriety or self-control, righteousness
or dealing rightly with our fellow men, godliness
or reverence for God, and hope or aspiration for
a nobler and diviner life. Or such as this:
" Pure religion and undefiled before God and
the Father is this, To visit the fatherless and

widows in their affliction, and to keep himself unspotted from the world." Then religion is purity and philanthropy. Or such as this: "Thou shalt love the Lord thy God with all thy heart, and with all thy soul, and with all thy might; . . . and thou shalt love thy neighbour as thyself." Then true religion is love toward God and love toward man. These and kindred definitions scattered through the Bible make it clear that, according to the Bible writers, religion is not a system of thought, a kind of ritual, or a church order, but a spiritual life. It is reverence toward God, the Father of all the living; repentance for sin and a turning away from it because it is loathsome to the soul; finding in the spiritual experience of other men something to which the soul answers and responds, and, preëminently, finding inspiration from the Bible as a book of spiritual experiences; seeing in Christ one worthy to follow, and having that kind of faith in Him which leads one to become a follower of Him; coming into fellowship with God, walking with Him, having His companionship, recognizing Him as a friend, living in His household as a child; feeling in one's self a certain quality that cannot die, and, because of that intense consciousness of undying quality, looking forward with hope beyond the grave for one's self and for one's loved ones. This is religion. It is the function of theology to give us such definition of God as it can ; but the reverence comes first, and the definition afterward. It is the function of theology to define sin, and to tell us, if it can, how it came into the world ; but the soul is first to turn with loathing from whatever it knows to be wrong, without waiting for definitions. It is the function of theology to explain, if it can, how it is that the Bible has been so preëminent in the history of the world, carrying with it everywhere the light of a nobler and diviner civilization ; but before that comes the answer of the human soul to the noble and inspiring words which the Bible utters. It is the function of theology to define, if it can, Christ's place in human history ; but before that comes the spirit which bows before Him, reveres Him, loves Him, follows Him. It is the function of theology to interpret, if it can, how sinful man can come into fellowship with an infinite and holy God ; but not until man has come into that fellowship can he define the coming. It is the function of theology to explain, if it can, how it is that the soul can go on in another life when this body has mingled with the common dust ; but before it can explain that phenomenon, the soul itself must be conscious of its immortal life and feel the divine and endless life within. My object, then, is not to make

the reader an evolutionist; it is not even to
revolutionize his theology; it is to show those
who are perplexed by doubt, whose minds have
seized upon evolution as a clue to the mystery
of life, and to whom that clue seems inconsistent with the religious teaching to which they
have been accustomed, that by a change in theology they may hold fast their faith in God,
their consciousness of sin, their fellowship with
Christ, their experience of pardon, their hope of
eternal life.

The theistic evolutionist believes in God, and
in a personal God, — that is, he believes in a
God who thinks and feels and wills; but he does
not believe in an embodied King, sitting on a
great white throne, remote, inaccessible, a God
afar off. He believes that God is truly in the
universe, and manifests Himself through all the
multifarious forces of nature; that what we call
laws of nature are the laws of God's own being;
that the activities of nature are the methods of
the divine; that God works out the creation
from within, thus revealing Himself by the con-
tinual forthputting of His wisdom and His
power. He thinks, therefore, that every day is
a creative day; that every spring God says
again, "Let there be light," and light comes
back to flood the world; that every spring He
again carpets the earth with grass, and brings

forth living creatures to inhabit the ocean, the earth, and the air ; that God always has been, is, and always will be, a speaking, working, revealing, disclosing God. This theology does not remove God further from him; it brings Him nearer. The evolutionist believes that in this process of self-manifestation God has wrought man, and that, so far as we know, man is the supreme fruit of God's creation, — certainly the supremest work yet wrought in the history of this globe. He believes that man is the product of that process which is at once evolution and divine manifestation, for all growth is the manifestation of God's own activity. He believes that man is God's own son, but God's son in the making. He looks upon the world as the factory where this making is going on ; it is full of dust and chips, and the statues are none of them finished. He sees man emerging from the animal condition, — half man, half animal. In Cole's picture of the expulsion from the garden, a great wall divides between the garden and the wilderness, — all flowers and fruits within, all weeds and thistles without. The evolutionist sees no such sharp line : the wilderness makes its incursion into the garden, and the garden makes its incursion into the wilderness, and the world is made up of tares and wheat growing together, in society, in the church, in every individual, —

each one of us part tare, part wheat; no man
so good that there is not some evil left in him,
no man so evil that there is not some seed of
good in him. He believes that sin enters every
human life, and the individual "falls" when
the animal nature predominates over the spiritual. He does not look back six thousand years
for a first sin. He does not throw the responsi-
bility of the transgression off upon poor, blun-
dering, sinful Adam; he recognizes that he
himself is carrying around the elements of a
sinful nature in himself. He reads again the
seventh chapter of Romans, and cries out with
Paul, In me — that is, in my flesh — I see no
good thing. This does not and will not make
sin seem less real, less awful, nor will it make
penitence less real, less sincere, less deep. The
evolutionist believes that God, who is the source
of all life, who is the one universal force, who
dwells in all nature, is brooding the human race.
He is the Father and the Mother of humanity.
Inspiration is the inbreathing of God, and God
breathes on all the souls He has ever made.
He is the Light that lighteth every man that
cometh into the world. There are two conceptions of pagan religion: one which regards all
pagan religions as the product of priestcraft,
devised by wicked men to get innocent men in
their power, — the fruits and products of the

devil; the other, which regards all religions as the reaching out of hands to God, the aspiration of ignorant and blinded souls for their Father. This is the belief of the evolutionist. This was the teaching of Paul, who, standing on Mars' Hill, and looking upon a city in which, an ancient satirist tells us, it is easier to find a god than a man, said to the assembled multitude, "Your own poets have borne witness that you are God's offspring; these idols are themselves evidences that you are searching after a God whom you do not know, and whom I have come to declare unto you." But though inspiration is as universal as the race, there is one people which has responded more quickly, answered more readily, and seen more clearly than any other, and the selected literature of that Hebrew race speaks with a power of inspiration with which no other literature speaks. How, then, does the inspiration of the Bible differ from the inspiration, we will say, of the sacred book of the Hindus? How it differs in *process* we do not know. How it differs in *result* we clearly see. Drop a peach-pit and an apple-seed in the ground: from one comes a peach, from the other an apple. What is the process that makes of one a peach-tree, of the other an apple-tree? No one knows. But no one thinks of saying the apple is a peach.

The evolutionist believes that God, who has

always been inspiring the human race, and always unveiling Himself to earnest human souls, when the human race had reached that stage of development in which it was possible for God to appear in a human life, and not be grossly and hopelessly misunderstood, did appear in a human life, that He might make perfect that revelation of Himself which He had been carrying on from the beginning. The controversy, more than a hundred years ago, in New England, between the Unitarian and the Orthodox turned on the nature of Christ. The Unitarian said, "He is not God, He is man;" the Orthodox said, "He is not man, He is God." Both seemed to agree that there was a clear antithesis between God and man; and that He could not be God if He were man, nor man if He were God. But the fundamental teaching of the Hebrew prophets from the beginning is this: that God made man in his own image. The difference between man and God is twofold: God is holy, man is sinful; God is infinite, man is finite. Conceive of a man who is perfectly holy, and he would be the image of God. Conceive of God coming into life and taking on finite proportions, and He would be a perfect man. For the difference between God and man is a difference not in essential nature. It is the fundamental teaching of the Bible that in their essential nature they are the same. The evolutionist, therefore, thinks of Christ, not as a strange, inexplicable God-man who was neither God nor man, not as a being who went through life doing some things as God and some things as man, but as God *in* man, God so perfectly possessing one unique human soul that in that soul we see reflected at once the image of God and the perfection of manhood. Christ is God manifest in the flesh; that is, such a manifestation of God as is possible in a human life.

The evolutionist thinks that the object of Christ's coming into the world is, not to release men from punishment, but to cleanse and purify them from sin. There is not to be found in either the Old Testament or the New Testament a single text which connects sacrifice in the one case or the suffering and passion of Christ in the other with the remission of punishment. The word " punishment " and the word " sacrifice " are not to be found so collated as to indicate that the sacrifice took the place of the penalty. Sacrifice is connected always with the remission of sin and the giving of new life. There is no way by which life can be quickened save by the imparting of life. Struggle for others is as integral a part of the doctrine of evolution as struggle for one's self. Sacrifice is the condition of life-giving.

The evolutionist, then, believes in God as the creator of the world, but God dwelling in the world and speaking through all its phenomena. He believes in sin as a violation of God's law; not of some edict issued by God at some remote time in history, but of the law of nature, and therefore of the law of God, and therefore of the law of man's own being. He believes in inspiration as a universal factor in human history, coming to its culmination in the literature of the Hebrew race. He believes in revelation; that is, in the unveiling of God to man, a gradual unveiling wrought in human experience, through the seers and prophets of all ages, but preëminently in Jesus Christ, God's well-beloved Son. He believes in Incarnation; that is, in the indwelling of God in his children, of which Incarnation the type and pattern is seen in Him who is at once the manifestation of God to man and the revelation to men of what humanity is to be when God's work in the world is done, — perfect God and perfect man, because God perfectly dwelling in a perfect man. He believes in atonement; that is, in a true reconciliation between God and man, making them at one through the Incarnation and Passion of Jesus Christ, who lived and suffered, not to relieve men from future torment, but to purify and perfect them in God's likeness by uniting them to God. He

believes in sacrifice, not as a penalty borne by
an innocent Sufferer for guilty man, — a doctrine for which he can find no authority, either
in Scripture or in life, — but as a laying down of
one's life in love that another may receive life.
He believes in redemption, not as a restoration
to a lost state of innocence, impossible to be
restored, but as a culmination of the long process when man shall be presented before his
Father without spot or wrinkle or blemish or
any such thing. He believes, not in propitiation
of an angry God by Another suffering to appease the Father's wrath, but in the perpetual
self-propitiation of the Father, whose mercy, going forth to redeem from sin, satisfies, as nothing
else could, the divine indignation against sin, by
abolishing it. He believes in immortality, not
as a mere endless existence, but as an undying
nature, which is superior to death, because it
shares with God, its Redeemer, the power of an
endless life. And he believes in religion, not as
a creed, a ritual, or a church order, which are at
best but the instruments of religion, but as self-
control, righteousness, reverence, hope, love, —
the life of God in the soul of man.

The Riverside Press

CAMBRIDGE, MASSACHUSETTS, U. S. A.
ELECTROTYPED AND PRINTED BY
H. O. HOUGHTON AND CO.

Lightning Source UK Ltd.
Milton Keynes UK
UKHW010626050121
376447UK00001B/12